*Moving
Through*

Moving Through
by Doug Rucker
Layout by Helane Freeman

Copyright © 2017 Doug Rucker
All rights reserved.

Doug Rucker
Vilimapubco
Malibu, CA
ruckerdoug@gmail.com

No part of this publication may be reproduced, distributed, or transmitted in any form or by any means, including photocopying, recording, or other electronic or mechanical methods, without the prior written permission of the publisher, except in the case of brief quotations embodied in critical reviews and certain other noncommercial uses permitted by copyright law.

For permission requests, sales to U.S. bookstores and wholesalers, or to inquire about quantity discounts, please contact the publisher at the email address above.

Printed in the United States of America

Library of Congress Control Number: 2017908313

ISBN 978-09988792-1-5

First Edition
10 9 8 7 6 5 4 3 2 1

Moving Through

TABLE OF CONTENTS

One

A CLEAR PICTURE – 6/66 .... *1*
VARIATION – 6/66. .... *2*
AGE OF ANXIETY – 10/66 .... *4*
INDUBITABLY UNSCRUPULOUS – 10/66. .... *5*
VERACITY TO KEEP – 11/6 .... *6*
SUN, RISING, SETTING – 11/66 .... *7*
OFFICE MOVE – 11/66. .... *9*

EXTRAS – 12/66. .... *10*
    Exactness. *10*
    Dim the Light *10*
    Man's Actions *10*
    Supper Bath. *11*
    Smoke *11*
    Sandwich *11*
    Two Parts. *11*
    Foggy Day *12*
    Mandy-Fats. *12*
    Decisive Rain. *12*
    Dead Planet. *12*
    'Twas Time to Change the Cat-box do. *13*

CONVERSATION – 12/66 .... *13*
NOW OR NEVER – 12/66 .... *15*
RUMBLEJACK THE HACK – 1/67 .... *16*
TIME TO GET YOURSELF – 1/67. .... *17*
MUSHROOM CLOUD – 3/67 .... *18*
HOPE – 3/67. .... *19*
LOVE? – 4/67 .... *20*

Two

I CRY – 4/67 .... *23*
INSANITY OF WAR – 4/67 .... *25*
STRANGE – 4/67 .... *25*
INSIGHT – 4/67 .... *26*
WILL TO LIVE – 4/67 .... *26*
EMERGENCE – 4/67 .... *27*
QUESTION – 5/67 .... *27*
QUALITY OF LIGHT – 5/67 .... *28*
THE RAREST GEM – 6/67 .... *29*
WAR – 6/67 .... *30*
MY GRIPE – 6/67 .... *31*
GOOD BUSINESS – 6/67 .... *31*
THE HAWK – 6/67 .... *33*
HARD AT WORK – 6/67 .... *34*

EXTRAS – 6/67 .... *35*
    Kitty *35*
    Impatience *35*
    Ticked-off at Ten *35*
    Essence *35*
    Supermarket *35*
    I Relate *36*
    The Real Me *36*
    Truth *36*
    What Right *36*

FEAR DREAM 67 – 6/67 .... *37*
SEAGULLS – 6/67 .... *38*
OUTSIDE – 7/67 .... *39*
WHILE I SLEEP – 7/67 .... *41*
NIGHT ACTIVITIES – 7/67 .... *42*

Three

IT'S ME – 7/67 .... *45*
SYMBOL OF LIFE – 7/67 .... *46*
REFLECTING TIME – 7/67 .... *47*
RELATIONSHIPS – 8/67 .... *49*
VACATION – 8/67 .... *51*
OLEANDERS – 8/67 .... *52*

PURIFICATION – 8/67	53
NOT THE EVERYDAY NEWS – 8/67	53
PARTICLE OF STAIN – 8/67	54
SOUND WAVES – 10/67	55
DO IT NOW – 10/67	56
WELCOME THOUGHT – 10/67	57
EXPLANATION – 10/67	58
THE BUTTERFLY – 10/67	59
SOUND OF LIFE – 12/67	60
THE SEARCH – 12/67	61

Four

THE AWAKENING – 4/73	65
FOREST THOUGHTS – 6/73	67
JOHN HENRY – 1/76	70
UNTIMELY WIND – 1/76	72
WHERE WILL I GO? – 1/76	73
THE ANT AND GOD – 1/76	74
EXTRAS – 2/76	74
Similarity	74
Poison Oak	74
Both Exhumed	75
Hate	75
Grass	75
Rollo's Directions	75
Flowers	76
Wife	76
Poetic Thought	76
Going Fast	76
Blueberry Sot	77
Tree in Rain	77
NOT POLITE – 2/76	78
COSMIC CLOCK – 2/76	79
BIRTH – 2/76	79
ANOTHER DAY – 2/76	81
I ROLL A ROCK – 2/76	83
MODERATION – 2/76	83
SOMEBODY ELSE – 2/76	84
EMANUEL – 2/76	84

TIME IS A PLACE – 2/76 .... *86*
WHERE ARE YOU, JOHN? – 2/76........................ *89*
THE UNIVERSE I SEE – 2/76 .... *90*
THE END RESULT – 2/76 .... *92*

Five

CONSIDER THIS – 2/76 .... *93*
LET'S STAY HOME – 2/76 .... *94*
GROWTH OF UNIVERSES – 2/76......................... *95*
FISH WITH A WISH – 2/76................................... *96*
WHAT I DID NOT FIND – 3/76 .... *96*
SLEEP – 3/76 .... *97*

EXTRAS – 3/76... *98*
    Stopped by Glass *98*
    Poor Passerby *98*
    Nonsense... *99*
    More Nonsense *99*
    Immaculate *99*
    Geronimo Choir *99*
    Ants *99*
    Sun... *100*

ON THE RAGGED EDGE – 3/76......................... *100*
BONY-RIDGE – 3/76 .... *101*
GO FIND YOURSELF – 3/76 .... *105*
THE CAVES – 3/76.. *105*
MEETING PLACE – 3/76 .... *107*
SHORTED OUT – 3/76 .... *108*
LOST SON – 3/76 .... *108*

Six

WHAT DO YOU SEE? – 3/76 .... *113*

EXTRAS – 4/76... *119*
    My Hope *119*
    Henry, Give it up............................ *119*
    Insult.. *120*
    Whimpering Willow........................ *120*
    Tree *120*

BREAK SERENELY ON THE DAY – 4/76 121
RAIN – 4/76 121
RAGGED DAYS – 4/76 122
THE SECRETS – 4/76 123
WHAT I SEE – 4/76 124
WHAT I SEE (2) – 4/76 125
SURPRISE – 4/76 126
LATE SUMMER – 4/76 127
SPIRIT OF MAN – 4/76 128
MOONLIGHT SHADOWS – 5/76 129

EXTRAS – 5/76 130
    Void is Black 130
    Stroboscope 130
    Shit-fit 131
    Mirrored Mind 131
    Repair Job 132
    Crackers 132

Seven

MORE RAIN – 7/76 135
I AM – 8/76 137
I SHALL BURST – 8/76 137
THIRD BRAIN DOWN – 8/76 138
I SIT IN BETWEEN – 8/76 139
BAOBOB – 8/76 140
BODY – 8/76 140
LATE AFTERNOON – 8/76 141
I WAIT – 8/76 143
HEAVEN – 8/76 144
READY TO STRIKE – 8/76 144
THE END – 8/76) 145
WHAT THE HELL AM I DOING HERE? – 12/76 146

EXTRAS – 12/76) 146
    Tendency 146
    Planting Seeds 147
    Caring 147
    What We Need 147
    Meaning? 148

```
EDGE OF THE DEAD – 12/77..........................148
HOT WIND – 12/76...................................149
WRITING IS A PRIVATE THING – 12/76.................150
CREATOR – 12/76....................................150
BLACKDOG – 2/77....................................151

EXTRAS – 2/77......................................152
         Yellow Sky................................152
         Stylistic Grace...........................152
         Coffee Anyone?............................152
         Mat's a Mil?..............................152
```

Eight

```
KORFU IMPRESSIONS – 2/77...........................155
MORE NOTHING – 2/77................................157
PLEASE DO IT – 2/77................................158
ONE TASK FINISHED – 2/77...........................159
I WISH TO DO IT MY WAY. – 2/77.....................161
WAITING FOR A DAUGHTER – 2/77......................162
CHILD'S PAINTING – 3/77............................163
PHOBOS AND DIEMOS – 3/77...........................164
THE ONE TO CALL HERSELF – 3/77.....................164
THE ANSWER – 4/77..................................165
DREAM, DISCOVERY, INSIGHT – 4/77...................167
I DRIFT IN A WAKING DREAM – 9/77...................168
UNDECIDED – 12/77..................................169
CHANGE – 12/77.....................................170
I DO GET UP – 12/77................................170
ELECTRIFIED – 12/77................................172

EXTRAS – 12/77.....................................173
         Strained Silence..........................173
         The Clock.................................173
         Which Category are You?...................173
         How to be Simple..........................174
         Poetry Reading by Ima Klutz...............174
         Head Down.................................174
         Heart.....................................175
         Roots and Shoots..........................175

SEEDS OF MYSELF – 12/77............................175
```

Nine

MING AND MANG – 12/77 .... *179*
CORRECT AND TRUE – 12/77 .... *181*
MY HEART SANG YOUR SONG – 12/77 .... *181*
DESPERATE – 2/78 .... *183*
DESTRUCTIVE HABITS – 2/78 .... *184*
WORDS WILL SAVE ME – 2/78 .... *184*
ON BEING FREE – 2/78 .... *185*
WITH APOLOGIES TO T. S. ELIOT – 2/78 .... *189*
HANGING IN – 2/78 .... *189*
FINITE SCHEME – 2/78 .... *190*
I SEE YOU TRY TO HEAL MY HEART – 2/78 .... *190*
CAN YOU LET ME GO? – 2/78 .... *192*
OH ANGUISH – 2/78 .... *193*
I CARE – 4/78 .... *194*
NO! – 4/78 .... *195*
GROWTH – 4/78 .... *195*
PARALLAX POWER – 4/78 .... *197*
IN DEADLY EARNEST – 4/78 .... *199*

Ten

EXTRAS – 4/78 .... *203*
    Shiver Me Timbers *203*
    Wow, Dad! *203*
    To Whom it May Concern *204*
    Brains of Paper *204*
    Finding Oneself *204*
    Trigger of Love *204*

NOW, IN DARK SHADOWS PLAYING – 5/78 .... *204*
GREENNESS AND DEATH – 5/78 .... *205*
MORE OF THE SAME – 5/78 .... *206*
FLOWING AND SINKING – 5/78 .... *207*
POUNDING – 5/78 .... *208*
EMERGING – 5/78 .... *209*
OVER AND UNDER – 5/78 .... *210*
WHISTLING – 5/78 .... *211*
WAITING – 5/78 .... *212*
QUIETLY I WAIT – 5/78 .... *212*
I REACH, AND REACHING, REACH – 5/78 .... *213*

GREEN STICK TREE – 5/78	*214*
THE ONLY – 5/78	*215*
IF I TRY – 5/78	*216*
I CLAIM IT MINE – 6/78	*217*
MUSIC TALK – 6/78	*218*
RARE GIFT – 6/78	*219*
WINNIE – 6/78	*220*
CLOSED – 6/78	*222*

Eleven

THANK GOD FOR THE DOVE – 6/78	*225*
LUCKY ONE – 6/78	*226*
DECISION TIME – 6/78	*227*
ONE MORE TIME – 6/78	*228*
I SHALL HAVE – 6/78	*229*
CLAIMING SPACES AGAIN – 6/78	*229*
SOME GREEN GRASS LEFT – 6/78	*230*
SCREW – 6/78	*231*
STONE – 6/78	*232*
FOUR SYMBOLS – 6/78	*233*
THE JOKE'S ON US – 6/78	*234*
ENOUGH – 6/78	*235*
THE OTHER SIDE – 6/78	*235*
THE CAT'S HOWL – 6/78	*236*
TOO, TOO, DEEP, DEEP – 6/78	*237*
FIRST STEP – 6/78	*238*
TIME TO BEGIN – 6/78	*239*
FREEDOM – 6/78	*239*
SAMENESS – 6/78	*240*
I KNOW ME – 6/78	*241*
MOON-SHATTERED – 6/78	*241*
WHERE SHALL I GO? – 6/78	*243*
EXTRAS – 6/78	*244*
Random Thoughts	*244*
Psychology	*244*
Knowledge	*244*

Twelve

SOMETHING MEANINGFUL, – 6/78	*247*
ANGELS SING SWEET SONGS – 6/78	*248*

THE HEARTSORE – 6/78	249
ART – 6/78	250
BLUE, THE GRASS OF THE HAPPIER HEART – 7/78	252
RAIN, WHERE ARE YOU? – 7/78	252
THE THOUGHT – 7/78	253
WHEN SHALL THE ...(Part 1) – 7/78	255
WHEN SHALL THE...(Part 2) – 7/78	260
WHEN SHALL THE...(Part 3) – 7/78	263
FEAR DREAM '78 – 7/78	264

Thirteen

WHAT SHE SAID (Part 1) – 7/78	267
WHAT SHE SAID (Part 2) – 7/78	270
MOON-TEARS – 7/78	270
ALIVE HE GOES INTO THE COFFIN – 7/78	271
THE FOREST HOLDS THE ANSWER – 7/78	272
HE PUT ME ON THE HOSE – 7/78	274
HASTY HEART – 7/78	275
PARTIAL INTERPRETATION, HASTY HEART – 7/78	276
LOVED LAND – 7/78	277
THE SMILING EYE – 7/78	277
WEEPING WILLOW AND THE BUSH – 7/78	279
GIVE ME A BREAK – 7/78	280
GERRARD HOUSE TRIP – 7/78	282
GORILLA DREAM – 8/78	283
SHOWER DREAM – 8/78	284
IN THE BRITTLE EVENING – 8/78	286

Fourteen

THE BURNING TREE – 9/78	289
SHADOW DANCE – 2/79	290
THE YOUNG MAN'S FANCY – 4/79	291
WHERE SHALL YOU GO? – 4/79	292
WORK TO DO – 4/79	292
LAMENT – 4/79	293
WHO SHALL BE THE WISER – 4/79	294
FACE OF GOD – 4/79	296
ON COMPROMISE – 5/79	297
MORE ANGUISH – 5/79	297
I FEEL THE SOLID EARTH – 6/79	298
I FEEL THE SOLID EARTH – (Completed) – 6/79	298

THE SPOTTED SNAKE – 6/79	299
MIDNIGHT THOUGHTS – 7/79	300
A LOVE POEM – 11/79	305
I FEEL THE LONG SILENCE – 12/79	306
WINTER RAINS – 2/80	307
THE LITTLE SHIP – 2/80	308
FROM THE TEAMING CENTER – 2/80	309
HE LEAPS – 3/80	310
THE VOICE IN THE MIST – 3/80	311

Fifteen

YOUR NATURAL RIGHT – 3/80	315
THE CROW – 3/80	316
SHALL I SEND YOU PLYWOOD – 3/80	317
ADORED – 3/80	318
CONTENT, FREE, FALLING – 3/80	319
THE NON-LEAPING CAT – 3/80	321
LOVE – 3/80	323
BECOMING WHOLE – 3/80	324
SONG OF THE PASSERBY – 3/80	324
MAGIC STONE – 3/80	325
SHOW TIME – 3/80	326
THUS, IT WILL EVER BE – 4/80	327
NOTES FROM THE UNCONSCIOUS – 4/80	329
GOOD "OLD" DAYS – 4/80	330

Sixteen

RELATIONS OF SIX – 4/80	335
IF SHE COULD COPE – 4/80	340
HAPPY BIRTHDAY – 4/80	341
SANTANA WIND – 4/80	342
THE JUMPER – 4/80	344
JOY OF MUSIC – 4/80	346
MARSH BIRDS – 4/80	347
THE ABANDONED TRUCK – 4/80	348
BOY IN BLUE JEANS – 4/80	350
THE BLUE PENCIL SPINNING – 4/80	351
ONE LANE ROAD – 4/80	352
THE WALKING CLOCK – 4/80	354
ONE SPIRIT – 4/80	356

Seventeen

PITH OFF – 4/80 .... *359*
THE WORDS ARRANGE THEMSELVES – 4/80 .... *361*
PATH DIVIDING – 5/80 .... *362*
POWER STAR – 5/80 .... *362*
TWO, I KNOW – 5/80 .... *363*
THE IMPOSSIBLE DREAM – 5/80 .... *364*
ON THE BRINK – 5/80 .... *364*
I HUM'DE DUM DUM – 9/80 .... *366*
GIVE ME SOME SKIN, PAL – 9/80 .... *366*
THROUGH THAT DOOR – 10/80 .... *367*
NO EXPECTATIONS – 10/80 .... *368*
THE BIG LESSON – 10/80 .... *369*
FREE? – 4/81 .... *370*
LONGING, SLEEPING, BEDDING, LOVING – 9/81 ..... *371*
THE CROAKING CRICKET – 9/81 .... *372*
CONVERSATION – 2/82 .... *373*
COTTON MAN DREAM – 2/82 .... *377*
THROUGH THE NOSE – 2/82 .... *378*

Eighteen

WHERE ARE YOU NOW? – 2/82 .... *381*
WHERE ARE YOU RAIN? – 2/82 .... *382*
UNCOMFORTABLE NIGHT – 2/82 .... *382*
IT DOESN'T SEEM QUITE REAL (DREAM) – 2/82 ..... *383*
WE CAN'T TALK – 2/82 .... *385*
HEAVY, HEAVY – 2/82 .... *386*
SWEET BIRD – 2/82 .... *386*
HOPE – 2/82 .... *386*
FOR MARGE – 2/82 .... *387*
CONVERSATION II – 2/82 .... *388*
WHO'S IN THERE – 2/82 .... *390*
FATE – 4/82 .... *390*
YOU SHOULDN'T HAVE DONE – 3/83 .... *394*
DOCTOR DIFFICULT – 3/83 .... *397*
WHEN I DANCE – 4/83 .... *398*
BEYOND RECKONING – 5/83 .... *399*
A PROTESTATION OF THE HIGHEST ORDER – 6/83 .... *400*
ON THE DEATH OF SUSAN SIERRA (Part 1) – 6/83 ..... *401*

Nineteen

SUSAN'S STUDIO – (Part 2) – 6/83 405
SUSAN'S WAKE – (Part 3) – 6/83 407
HOW I FELT – (Part 4) – 6/83 408
DANCING WITH DEB – (Part 5) – 6/83 409
DANCE – 6/83 413
SEARCH – 6/83 414
END OF THE ROAD – 6/83 417
INDESCRETION – 6/83 419
FOOD FOR THE ANCIENT GREEK – 8/83 420
LISA RUSCHEK – 8/83 421

Twenty

ROARK – 8/83 425
INSTANT SPACE – 11/83 427
POSSIBLE TO LIVE – 1/84 428
I WRITE – 1/84 429
YOUPA GOUPA – 1/84 430
THE SEED – 4/84 431
YOU GOT ME THINKING – 5/84 432

EXTRAS – 7/84 433
    Which Record for You? 433
    Possums 433
    You Know 433
    Don't be Afraid 434
    From the Shore, the Roar 434
    Thinking Bird's Dog 434

UNRELATED THOUGHTS – 8/84 435
LEAVES IN THE GARDEN – 8/84 436
I WISH – 8/84 437
THE WINDS THEY CAME A-WHISTLING – 8/84 439
THINK ON, FAIR LILY – 8/84 440

EXTRAS – 8/84 441
    I Have A 441
    Born of the Air 442

I SAVOR – 8/84 .... *442*
SOMETIMES RAIN – 8/84 .... *443*

Twenty-one

FIRST MEMORY – 9/84 .... *447*
IMAGINED MEMORY – 9/84 .... *449*
PARTS OF ME I'LL KEEP – 9/84 .... *450*
MATCHING STARS – 9/84 .... *451*

EXTRAS – 9/84 .... *453*
    Sunflower *453*
    My Reflection *453*
    My True Love's Nose *453*
    TV Set *453*
    The Ocean *454*
    No Choice *454*
    Drying Dew *454*
    To Know the Leaf *454*
    Pickles *454*
    Cat's Fleas *454*

NOTHING – 9/84 .... *455*
A DREAM – 9/84 .... *456*
FISH LAKE – 9/84 .... *457*
AN EQUALITY – 9/84 .... *458*
I WRITE – 9/84 .... *459*
TELEPHONES – 10/84 .... *461*
I LISTEN FOR RUMBLINGS – 11/84 .... *462*
ODE TO GLOOM – 12/84 .... *463*
THE WOLF AND I – 12/84 .... *464*

Foreword

*T*hese are about all of my poetic efforts, from the first to the last. My daughters have told me I'm a talkative Guru who sees all, knows all, tells all. They say that in fun, but they may be serious. Guess I'll cop out. It does seem I'm that.

This is a collection of stuff that went through my head while trying to figure things out. No! I wasn't always aware I was not perfect. I just thought so when I was younger. I intended to have the perfect family, everyone loving, artistic, talented, with intelligence and passion. When things got difficult, unhappily I began to awaken. Am I perfect now? No! I don't think so! But I believe I'm closer than before. I credit the passage of time and automatic writing inherent in poetry with that.

If I didn't make this collection, I visualized all my efforts, the whole kit and caboodle, would wind up a bunch of papers eventually thrown out with the trash. However, I reasoned, it's more difficult to lose something carefully organized inside a cover, like a book. It's easier to keep books than old papers. I should know, I have a bunch of mother's old notebooks I'm dreading going through.

In a trip through a troubled marriaige, you will find humor, *(I can't get up to do my work, 'cause kitty's on my leg.)* pathos, dreams, egotism, *(Dim the light, it's just too bright, it's coming right from me!")* imagined conversations, nonsense, philosophy, *(In a single tick of the cosmic clock, I'm strata!)* psychology, love, regret, dictionary poems, automatic writing, and a host of other weird absurdities. Hope you like it. It's life!

The statement of the collection is: ideas about anything and everything happening in life and what I thought about them. Being objective about the work, I can't believe I deliberated on all those topics. You may be observing the thoughts of <u>any</u> man, however I <u>am</u> the any-man and I did write them down for us to see. It is my hope you will be delighted, saddened, share love and laughter with me, and enjoy the totality of any-man's experience.

About the drawings: I did about 150 drawings in a 4 month period at the end of 1979 and beginning of 1980. Marge, whom I'd met early in 1976, was studying Art Therapy at Loyola University, and I got the idea that I would try some Art Therapy on myself. I was tired of thinking and came to the wonderful idea of doing drawings with no possible thought whatsoever. I call them my *No Think* drawings. When I recently looked at them, I tried to piece together their exact meaning. Going deep within myself, I discovered I haven't the faintest idea of what the *No Think* drawings mean. I conjecture I was drawing the inside of my mind and being. I was doing soul-drawings. *(Or were they doodles?)* Ever ask yourself what you are <u>really</u> about? For me, the *No Think* drawings are what <u>I'm</u> <u>really</u> about. Now neither of us know. You know the sound of two hands clapping. What is the sound of one hand clapping?   Doug

Moving Through

One

A CLEAR PICTURE *6/66*

Your attitude determines
the cleanliness of the window
through which you see the light of day.
For a cleaner window
you must first know
the window is dirty.
You may discover the window is dirty if
past fortune allows you to sense it,
or you are convinced by outer forces,
agents of the brighter light,
that it is.
You will clean that window
to the degree you are dissatisfied.
Study the relativity of all things.
A little each day will do the job.

And yet, I can't do it.
The pain is insufficient.
I haven't the meagerest curiosity.

My window is shady at best,
or dark,
or encrusted,
or all three.
Must I too, wait for agents?
Shall I recognize them?
Vainly hope, perhaps,
for some latent curiosity to save me?

Perhaps my window, ever dirtier,
will cause the pain to make me clean.
Shall I then only scrub
'til pain is bearable again?

And what if my real self,
my it,
is more satisfied, unsatisfied?
Can I undo that too?
Perhaps we are as Bhuddist's say,
the river,
deep and shallow,
cool and warm.

VARIATION   6/66
(On a Rick Davidson paragraph - poem called to my love.*)*

"...ago eleventh higher
invited fifteenth tower
kin-folks birthday,
greeted thirteen evils,
themselves,
sever the hundred circles..."

(above out of context)

Variation:

Not long ago
the situation was critical,
insurmountable and too late.
Not too late if acted quickly.
Did not act.

The action imperative.
A yes was *must*.
No time for *no*.
Quickly, quickly, or too late.
Why did I not?
It passed.
Perhaps it was critical.
Perhaps not at all.
I forget.

Here is a birthday party,
balloons and hats,
food and family members.
Laughter and children noises.
Confusion, animated.
Sunshine.
Hot.
Shiny.
Tired.

Sun up – sun down.
Sun up – sun down.
Sun up – sun down.
Sun up – sun down.
Sun up – sun down.
What did I do five sun-ups ago?

Crisis.
Contentment.
Tears.
A special solid feeling
after producing something worthwhile.

AGE OF ANXIETY *10/66*

I get up early.
The hostile sun
declares the day's vitality.

My being rises to my throat
and spreads to the extremities
filling every void with juice.
My eyes with tears ingested,
hands strong with blood and warm,
certify it will be *fight* today, not *flight*.

But who or what?
Nothing is there.

Shall I fight my financial situation,
injustice, poverty, world problems,
everything not right?

My heart beats now
ready for the crisis.
It is here, I feel it.

I shall predominate, by God, this time!
I can do it!
I'll fight it!

Where is it?

INDUBITABLY UNSCRUPULOUS ***10/66***

*I*ndubitably unscrupulous
he was and that was that!
He stole her sky-blue XKE
her wine, her coat, her hat.
Took them all and drove away,
to Boise, Hartford, Mandalay,
casting tidbits as he went
wildly to the wind.

Then one day his meager purse,
lightened by his wicked spree,
forced a plan unto him thus,
surreptitiously.

Returning to that very place,
disguising then, his evil face,
set up a stand where he might meet
that self-same girl upon the street.

And when at last, she came by
inquiring what he had for sale,
he looked her squarely in the eye
and this will end my tale.

Sold her back, her coat, her hat,
her XKE with right rear flat,
a coffee cup and donut, too,
expired ticket to the zoo,
a pill that's fun to take for fat,
all this without a fuss.

This, he was and that was that,
indubitably unscrupulous.

VERACITY TO KEEP

The sun with tired rays was growing old.
The universe was aging.
The earth was cold, encrusted now,
and stratified with life's debris.

The moon was gone,
deflected from her course,
upon and endless journey through the stars,
and nights were dark and frozen in a massive block.
This was not a sudden thing,
but several trillion years had passed
since all the vegetation died
and mankind reached its end.

And now the crippled planet
limped along with one lost eye,
the other, lifeless, apathetic,
mother-source no more.

One hundred million light years close
another planetary system,
solid, whirling, vital force,
evolved the miracle of growth.
Bathed in sunshine,
tall green grass,
decisive rain and then the wind
that combed and clarified the night,

with animals of every kind,
in every sense alive,
now contented, now in fear,
now with offspring, purpose clear,
procreated,
lived their lives a million-fold.

Slowly then, but quickly, too,
time recorded age.

Ever forward, never stopped,
completing every phase,
worked its dying transformation,

dried the planet, froze her, shrunk her,
cast her farther into space.
Forgotten record file out there
memory bank of what took place.

*(Life illumined brilliant,
like sight once lost
regained for just an instant,
then forever gone.)*

For everywhere,
add time to time,
the cycle makes its sweep.
This one lives while that one dies.
(Veracity to keep.)

SUN, RISING, SETTING   *11/66*

The sun is rising.
Sit there.
Watch it.

Our only mother brings her gift.
A fresh beginning.
How many have I seen?
And through the day
she's always there,
though my concentration's here,
I feel her presence
as well being.
Now she makes that final sweep.

The sun is setting.
Sit there.
Watch it.

How many have you seen?
Grayish cloud
with growing whiteness
gains the ultimate in pink,
then fades.

Force and power of the sun,
single out a mountainside.
A light, bright green
deepens in a rosy shade.

Reflected atmospheric cloud
calmly stimulates the air
and then that yellow aura,
strange,
that sends my soul to netherland
and fourth dimension.

Am I here?
And If so, why?

Have I just died?
Or just arrived?
Clearly, I'm a part.

Colors purple, green and golden,
rich beyond experience,
pervades the air, surrounding land,
my body, too,
nothing as a thought,
everything as in a dream.

All the clouds a-blazing orange.
Black one there in fish disguise,
and there a silver barracuda,
basking thinly, ten miles long.
And then a cooler breeze creates a star.

By intimate degrees the night is born
with soft nocturnal sounds and sights
charged with power all its own
to last 'til rising time again.

OFFICE MOVE *11/66*

This entire stack shall go.
I'll consider this.
Things like that go over there.
This, I'll never miss.

So it goes, all day long,
the will is up to get it done.
The office shall be moved today
by setting of the sun.
My feelings grasp at hazy wisps
of gently moving air,
attempt to tell me, fruitlessly,
what is left of all that time,
those working years,
for me to take along.
The answer's there,
there is no doubt,
time to carry this one out,
next will be the chair.

Shall my future years be good?
The thought arrives, concerned.
Again the wispy feelings
try in vain to speak.

They flutter there
and shudder there,
intelligent but dumb.

And should I really care?
Immense relief, this salty thought,
it's now I have with juice to spare.
The point-blank thing is <u>now!</u>
What did take place and shall take place,
I know just can't be there.

The box in hand,
a solid grasp,
careful now,
and feel the stair.

EXTRAS *12/66*

Exactness

How exact
is exact?
Consider tact.
It's a fact
that its packed
with exact
not intact.

> ***Dim the light***
>
> **D**im the light,
> its just too bright,
> its coming right from me.

Man's Actions

A man becomes his actions
whether he agrees with them or not.

Supper Bath

Now their heads are among the toys
and now they're on their knees,
with piercing shouts and grimaces
and lively swirling back and forth.
The kinesthetic sense alive,
the overflowing heart,
makes the scene delightful
to a tired father's eyes.

Smoke

Smoke from the vase
slithers up
dissolves and reappears.
Hypnotic in its undulation.
Unreal, as in a dream.

Sandwich

A peanut butter sandwich
and a glass of Sal-Hepatica.

Two Parts

Two parts,
I find,
there are.
(We won't go far.)
One is: Get the work.
Two is: Do the work.
To get the work,
you must have done the work.
And so,
you know,
around we go.

Foggy Day

Brightened by the breaking wave,
the foggy day returns to gray,

Mandy-Fats

I'm in this other room you see,
and hear this awful WUNK!
I know it must be Mandy-Fats
that's fallen from her bunk.
And then I hear this cry and run
to see what I can do.
And half-way there I meet her
on her way to see me, too.
Everything's OK except for
just a small blue knob.
And all she needs is comfort
and a great big ice-cream blob.
And then I put her back to stay,
I hope, I hope, I hope.
To prevent her fall again this time,
I tie her with a rope.
Now all is peace
and I can drink my coffee,
eat my roll.
I dash the coffee down the sink.
Gosh darn it! It's too cold!

Decisive Rain

Decisive rain and then the wind
that combed and clarified the night.

Dead Planet

Forgotten record file out there,
memory bank of what took place.

Time to Change the Cat-box do.

'Twas time to change the cat-box do,
I picked it from the floor.
The box in tippy balance,
one hand to reach the door.
Disbelief on seeing fall,
settled on my face,
the sand and do on jamb and shoe
putrefied the place.
Obscenities came to mind,
and new vows by the score,
rid ourselves the stinky cats
and clean the stinky floor.

CONVERSATION *12/66*

One o'clock.
The bulb above the table swayed
and tinked against the beaded string.
Like super rubber balls,
the nimble conversation
bounced and banged and ricocheted
across the empty cups.

One fell in my drink
and spinning, stayed.
One bruised me on the head.

Another, rolling fast, ran out the door
and down the steps to smash a bottle far away.

Charged with personality,
perfect, to the point,
the punched out P's

and tongue-tipped T's,
with points projected,
driven home,
and gesture shadows on the wall.
Conviction crammed the tongue and teeth
demanding to be freed.
Resolves were made and feelings felt,
and uppermost, the juice inside
made living more alive.

Two o'clock.
The bulb above the table, motionless, like ice.
The paralytic beaded string hanging there, precise.

The atmosphere yet pungent
with the spoken word and thought,
cleared the while the table cleared
in the stillness of the night.

What of those words,
those punchy P's and tonguey T's,
those pregnant verbal thoughts
that occupied the air?
Where are they now?

Absorbed by all the universe and gone?
Off our chest, expressed?
Into our heads to work a change
when we are down to rest?

Shall we act on what we said?
Or was what we said, the act?

NOW OR NEVER *12/66*

*I*f you really don't care, will you ever?
Is it true that it's now or it's never?

And your work, you confess,
brilliantly a mess,

will have to go for less
or for nothing?

Can you lie down and sleep
and never count sheep?

Can you sleep away the night
and never have to fight.

Or does your conscience rise
and dance before your eyes,

until the morning crow
surprises you with snow.

Snow?

Time to stay in bed.
Rest my weary head.

Tomorrow's very near.
Ridiculous to fear.

Sleep awhile and rest.
Today is not the test.

And after such a night,
sleep is really right.

Such a blissful body, this.
Not a thing I'd want to miss.

Covers toasty, warm, secure,
relaxed and floating, I demure.
I really care right now, you know,
when barometers are low,

and I, a lightly dozing feather.
It's true! It's now or never!

RUMBLEJACK, THE HACK *1/67*

*R*umblejack, the hack,
took another tack
and rifled, quickly, through his mind
to see what topics he could find
to interest sleepy Mack.

"Killer Mack," the Yak, he was,
the one who always duped the *"fuz"*,
the one who broke the latch in two
the day the bear escaped the zoo
and mauled his second cuz'.

And now the Mack was drowsy.
The escape had just been lousy.
He'd leased the hack of Rumblejack
and called him *"frowsey, blowsey!"*

And now the only hope for Jack
lay only in his talking knack.
to talk the Killer Yak to sleep,
to steal his gun without a peep,
and try to get on back.

"Twas nineteen hundred twenty-two, the year that I was one..." A quiet buzz was heard behind,
the Yak had dropped his gun.
The *"Killer-boy"* was sleeping sound
and in a fetal pose, and Rumblejack
could scarcely see the tip of *"Killer's"* nose
from out the huge anatomy that must have weighed a ton.

So back he drove him to the zoo.
You should have heard the keepers boo.
Yes, Rumblejack brought back the Yak
and plopped him, heavily, in his sack,
while far away, a cow went .....! *(Forget it.)*

TIME TO GET YOURSELF   *1/67*

Appleberry pie and blueberry gumbo.
Pile it up high so it's really a jumbo,
and gobble it down and make myself sick.
Funny what makes people tick.
Light up a Lucky and deeply inhale
and do it again until I am pale.
A method, unconscious, to pay myself back,
for things I know I lack.

Get a little foggy when it's five o'clock at night
and after dinner, what the hell, get a little tight.
A way to duck existence, I know it to be true.
Picture of a normal life that's just a little blue.

And when I'm feeling cranky and a cold is on its way,
I'll tell everyone about it and consider it all day.
It's the way I'm really happy, though I can't think why.
I gaze into my coffee and give a little sigh.
For things I can't forgive myself,
a balance must I seek.
Now's the time to get myself.
Come on now, don't be weak.

MUSHROOM CLOUD 3/67

I equals MC squared,
and how have you fared?
All this by way of excuse
to show our head's in a noose.

The point of man's greatest achievement
is the point of man's greatest bereavement.

HOPE *3/67*

If I mingle with the masters of the beat,
and mess around those maulers of the ear,
and sing along and swing around the sound,
then everyone'll think I've been around.

If I bang about in numbers with my car,
and speed among the freeways of the town,
and drag my brother members at the stop,
then everyone'll know I've reached the top.
If I try the latest pill-fad on the scene,
and show them I am fearless, unafraid,
and swallow down and take a little trip,
there isn't any question that I'm hip.

But what will happen later on in years?
Does hipster life appeal at sixty-five?
The answer I don't know, I'm sure,
and now I couldn't care.

To work a change at this late date,
to purge myself of all the hate,
to mend a former painful life,
prepare the root for sturdy growth,
is quite a job, indeed.

And chances are it won't be done.
But chances are it will.

LOVE?

*E*xpect our child
to go to bed.
Away he goes.
He knows our love.
He has it, too.

Expect politeness,
diligence and truth,
and he'll deliver,
never fear,
for *love's* the way.

So why not
expect our child
to die for us?
It's the law.
We must obey.

Expect our child to kill.
Aren't other children killing him
in honor's name,
which it is not?

And on the field,
in grim-gray light
and terrified
before he dies
(just half our age)
may never know,
or knows the truth.

The ultimate betrayal
by those he loved
who loved him most.

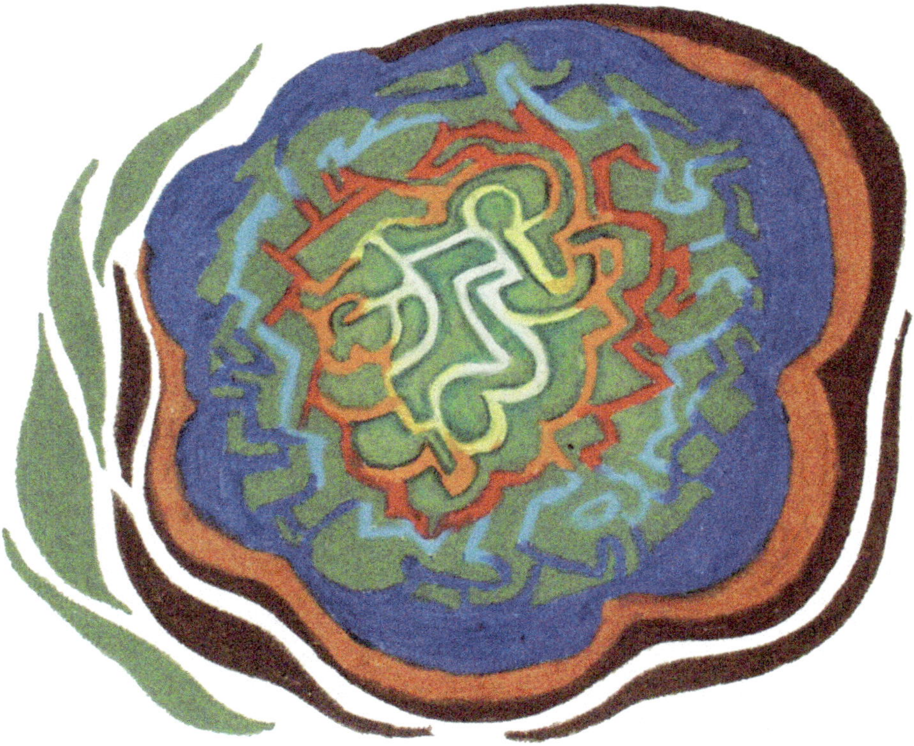

Two

I CRY   ***4/67***

*I*n this country
it is considered
unmanly to cry,
so I do not.

But were I honest,
(and I intend to be)

I would admit
I'd like to cry,
though I do not.

Instead I capture thoughts
and set them here,
for they are tears
when I am dry.

But even this,
I've come to know,
is not considered right.

To be a man
you kill a deer
(a blast between the eyes)
or smoke a fag,
or drink a lot,
or go to war,
obey the law,
kill a mother's son.
(For Christ?)

Ah! There I go,
venting feelings
men conceal.

Though deep inside
I am sure
we all would like to cry.

And since we can't,
it bottles up,
eventually explodes
in anger, acts of violence,
the vain attempt
to solve it all by force.

These acts of which
are just the things
compelling me now to write.

I should be shedding tears.

INSANITY OF WAR *4/67*

The sons protest the war.
They like this life as we do, too.
And yet I hear them called insane
    by those who send
    their only sons,
    their only seed,
    their only life
    to do a deed and have it done,
destroy the human race.

STRANGE *4/67*

A mouth and nose
to taste and smell
and ears to hear the sound.
Skin and fingers,
sense of touch,
and eyes to see around.

INSIGHT   4/67

I wonder.
I'm aware,
as time stands still
and I go by,
that old are young,
and strain is strain.
That shock is shock,
and smells are sweet
right now as then,
and love is love
at any time,
though more intense each day.

WILL TO LIVE   4/67

I saw an old man cry today,
his wife no more the mate she was.
Controlled himself and realized,
consciously or no,
that two and only two
(for him)
choices now remained.
The first one death,
a hollow hole.
The second equal to the first,
though backed with hope,
to take another step.

EMERGENCE 4/67

How is it
man emerges
from everlasting darkness
into this wondrous life
of things so grand
as sky and land,
and things as grand
as violets
in shade of forests,
unexplored,
and then returns,
in time, too short,
to everlasting darkness
once again?

QUESTION 5/67

My daughter fair,
picked from the air
and asked me bold and true,
"How is we are here?"
When I replied,
(the truth inside)
I didn't really know.

She said,
SHE DID!
She thought she knew.

*"We just grew,
and that was that,
a simple fact."*

Miraculous
chemical
combinations.

Infinite
temperature
variations.

We just grew
and that was that.
My psyche
split in two.

And round I went
to who made God,
and who made Him,
and who made Him
and Him?

QUALITY OF LIGHT *5/67*

*I*t's late at night,
you've studied hard,
your breath the only sound.
A brilliant book,
your tired eyes,
and darkness all around.

THE RAREST GEM *6/67*

*T*ake the rarest gem,
the you that's really you,
and capsule it in wax.

Dull the brightness,
kill the glare,
stop the rays from shining through.

Simulated commonplace
fraudulently posed.

Bogus mediocrity
carefully exposed.

And when you die,
the gem intact,
what is it that you've done?

Gazelle, shelf-shackled,
on the plain,
never leaping free.

Eagle in the dove's domain,
wings, self-clipped,
and eating hay.

*(Though concealment was your aim,
we saw you, all the same.)*

Cannibalistic plant
feeding on its roots,
unhappy in its pain.

Apologetic rose,
touched up,
standing in the rain.

And so the double death,
'twas not for friends,
'twas not for self.

A circumstantial crime!

Feel no regret.
It's not your fault.
I am you.
I did the same.

WAR   *6/67*

A dying tree without a seed.
Father, kill them off and don't look back!
A heart that aches with dread.
Menopausal mother crying.
All sons dead.

MY GRIPE *6/67*

The old grind
is like eating the rind.
Instead of the meat,
it's the gristle I eat.
Instead of enjoyment,
I maintain employment.
Instead of my life,
I just get the knife,
with a twist.
But I'm lucky to live in America.

GOOD BUSINESS *6/67*

It is essential in business
you like yourself,
for if you do not,

your work,
the extension of you,
will pall and fade away,
as you will, too.

Who can sell what they don't like,
much less hate?
No enthusiasm flows.
Joyous overtones are gone.
And so what fearful thoughts
race through your client's head?

If you are dull
and shift your eyes
and stand on this foot,
then on that,
how can he come alive or be enthused,
sell your idea *(really his)*
to banker, friend or wife?

He's been robbed!
He's bought no joy!
(Really moneys only worth.)

Better you had never met,
but gone your separate ways,
he to Heaven,
you to Hell.

For *"love yourself"*
means *"love your work"*
and men will love your work and you,
(and themselves)
which is essential to business.

THE HAWK

I went with him
over the hills.
The hawk,
gliding easily,
riding the breeze,
steady as a thousand years,
falling, rising,
effortlessly.

Realization struck the blow,
for crushed within his horny jaw,
strangled, eyes a-bulge,
must have been a fledgling.
I did not see.
But diving, frantic,
spinning flight in crazy strings,
one tenth the size,
an ineffective mother-bird
attacked the hawk.

Swooped and dove
with streaming eyes,
fighting currents and the hawk,
sick with grief,
played her futile game.

The steady hawk as he flew,
twitched a steely eye
and would have said,
had he been me,
(for I am both, you see)

"Mother, go your way.
This one's mine.
A meal to eat
to last me out the day."
And straight away
increased his speed,
rode another current up
and disappeared behind a hill.

HARD AT WORK   6/67

I have work to do,
but I don't want to.
I'm not hungry,
but it won't be long
'til I can eat,
avoid my work,
munch a little something down.
Perhaps I'll pick my teeth
and think of other things,
engage in conversation,
remember calls I have to make,
distract myself in other ways,
in best of conscience, don't you see,
because of *"coffee-time."*
I do wish I were hungry.

EXTRAS

Kitty

I can't get up to do my work
'cause kitty's on my leg.

Impatience

Stoplights take longer
when its hot.

Ticked-off at Ten

Three little children under six.
Suicidal mother in a fix.

Essence

I love my life.
I love my wife.
Because I do,
she does too.

Supermarket

Supermarket,
meat department,
is it really true?

Fluorescent buzz.
I never wuz.
The meat and I are blue.

I Relate

*M*y relationship
to relativists
is relative.

The Real Me

A quiet thrill
runs through me now
as I receive adoring looks
from all my fine associates
as they approve
with glowing eye
the ME
I've worked so hard to be
that isn't me at all.

Truth

*T*here's not a tree
so badly bent
could not, in years
send off the shoots
so glistening green
and full of sap
towards the morning sun.

What Right

*W*hat right have we
to ask our sons
to give away
the gift of life
in honor's name
which it is not?

FEAR DREAM 67 *6/67*

Castles far away,
snugly in the hills,
comfortable, serene,
surrounded by the deepest green,
the strangest green,
near a lake as blue or bluer than the sky.
Brilliant noonday sun
fuses all with life.
The birds from tree to tree,
the fox,
the man,
the woman.
Listen carefully.
Hear grass growing,
    breath of trees,
      quiet insistence,
    earth-sound,
    no sound.

Giant hawks!
Wings a mile wide,
hurtle on the scene.
Blot out the sky.
Blot out the castle.
Blot out the lake,
    the living things.

Paralyzed, I freeze.
Muscles tied, bound,
a thousand cords around.

Fear dream 67.
Hope I go to heaven.

SEAGULLS 6/67

*O*ver the board,
completely lost,
roaming within my brain.

Then intrusion
drifting down.
The strangest sound
invades my world.
Hens or birds
crowing, cackling far away?

Eyes in focus, zero in.
I walk outside.

Away so high,
swarming against the sky,
in purest joy,
900 seagulls soar,
    hover
    shoot,
in spiral dives,
daring turns,
quick ascents.

With varied speeds,
and various shades,
    now gray,
    now white,
    now black,
their wings spread out,
they catch the rays,
twist about,
and shut them out,

higher
higher.

Tiny salt and pepper dots.
Agitated motion
falling into heaven.

Then calling noises indistinct,
they fade against a thundercloud
billowing against the blue.
Euphoria of gulls,
ever higher,
soon are out of sight.

Only I remain,
motionless,
feet on the ground,
rising with them still.

OUTSIDE 7/67

*O*utside! Outside!
Horizon level,
mounding up,
leaping at the sky,
one, two, three or more,
they come.

Paddle out
straight away!
Instantly I'm tired.
Heart pounding.

Will I take it?
Will I make it?
Number one's the easy one,
but if I miss, I'm caught inside.
Number two's the one to watch,
the one to catch if mettle's there.

Up and over number one,
and here comes shoulder number two,
pounding white and blue.
Turn and paddle twice!
    DECIDE!
      Heart and soul!
      All the way,
      or not at all!
There's the place to go!
And then I drop.
My surfboard drops.
      My body drops.
      The world drops.
      My guts remain upstairs.

The board takes hold, solidifies.
(It may close out!)
I run to the nose.
I feel the surge.
I *am* the force of the wave,
adrenaline charged,
one with God
and moving fast.

WHILE I SLEEP *7/67*

I think I'll go to bed
and read awhile tonight.
And after endless words,
drifting, drowsy, eyelids down,
I'll put away my book,
roll over, stomach-wise,
stretch my feet, my back, my arms,
and quickly fall
in deep,
deep,
sleep.

Not to dream.
Not to be aware.
Miraculous personage, me,
man, woman.
Repairing, adjusting,
tuning my body,
perpetual, motion-like,
cleaning the wastes,
grooming, caring, detailing.
As I sleep, someone,
something takes good care,
(not me)
for when I wake,

I'm born again; seeing better,
hearing better,
calm,
ready for changes the new day brings.

I am grateful.
I have no pain.
My organism is functioning.
On to new things.

NIGHT ACTIVITIES

Late at night, after one.
Quietly,
the stair-treads take my brush.
A natural stain,
a balmy night.
My dog beside me sleeping, calm.
Perhaps a little stereo
to while away the time.

Crickets chirping far away.
And lightly now, a breeze disturbs outside,
comes, blows warm and fades away.
No music!
It's good to listen to: paint brushes
                         night crickets
                         breezes,
                         sleeping sounds,
movements of my shoes against the stairs.
      Feel the tired in my arm.
      It's there. It's tired.
      It feels good to feel.

The night is sweet.
Not really silent.
Really quite musical.
Really filled with life,
the truest high fidelity

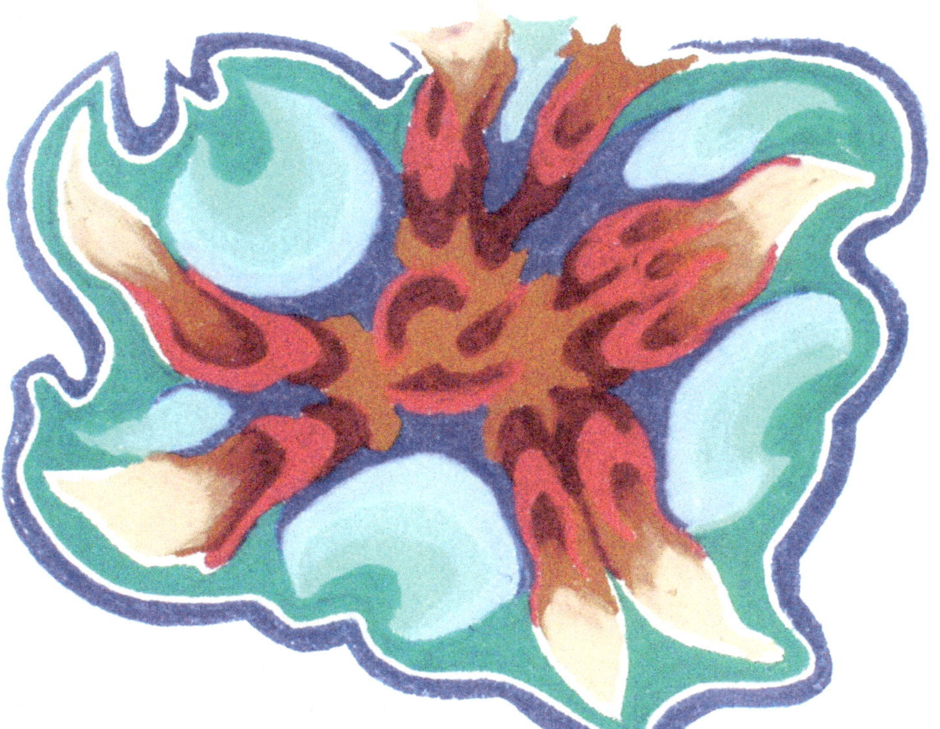

Three

IT'S ME 7/67

I find I'm <u>not</u> concerned *"out there."*
I am concerned *"<u>right here</u>."*
For this is the spot
where <u>I</u> take place.
Ego as big as the whole outdoors,
over the canyon rim it soars.
Another time will come, perhaps,
to think *"out there"* of things.

Right now it's <u>here</u> I'll contemplate,
and think of things for *ME*.
Wrapped in Holy Aura bright,
absolutely sure I'm right,
secure in fantasy.

SYMBOL OF LIFE

I love tender greenish shoots,
bending toward the sun.
Symbol of life,
hope,
adventure,
love,
and all good things.
And most of all,
best of all,
the flower,
in whatever shape,
since all are best
and only judged
in light of all the rest.
And then the seed.
I think of manzanita nuts,
hard and round,
explosive packed,
rolling on the softened earth,
searching out the proper hole
in which to drop and stay,
safe from rain,
and wind,
and birds,
and prowling things.
Waiting for its time.
Then silently,
when mortals look the other way,
a slender, white and tender shoot
(don't underestimate its strength)
divides the shell.
A hungry, moisture-seeking tendril
sinks down deep.

The required time passes
(evidently not a change)
until that special day,
as our planet, spinning 'round,
reveals the morning sun,
exposes glistening dew,
and all living things,
I discover dirt dislodged.
A tender manzanita shoot
sloping, greenly, toward the sun,
symbol *(to me)* of life ,
with all its connotations.

REFLECTING TIME 7/67

The days work over,
I sit down.
Miraculous!
"All's quiet on the western front."
Kids are busy.
Mom's in the garden.
Remote fan's all I hear.

Elbow on the table,
hand on jaw,
I write. *(Look outside.)*
Dusk!
Rolling, jagged,
intermittent mountain range.
Hillsides green and brown,
littered table, all around,
portion of my car in view,
crickets faint, far away.

Crickets!

And what are we to them?
And what are they to us?
The same, I'd say.

Green mold on our planet, crusting.
White, the polar cap descends,
recedes and comes again.
Green and white.
Green and white.
A million times or more,
'til quickly, quietly,
(midway in eternity)
our earthen planet fractures up.
Splits away.
Floats in fragments into space,
ever farther, unrelated.
Separated!
Seeking other solid states
of which to become a part.

And soon this earth
and we, mankind,
are scattered in our galaxy.

But even galaxies
made up of time
and planets such as ours,
and other matter not dissimilar,
grow old.
Break up.
Disintegrate.
As in a gas expanding,
filling the unfillable.
Then we, our earth,
our galaxy, join all the heavenly bodies,
and everything is made of everything.

. . .

So what does <u>this</u> have to do with wars?
Hemingway says,
if we destroy others,
we destroy ourselves,
for we and the enemy are mankind.

Is this really true?
Yes and no!
For nothing is destroyed,
just once removed,
and once removed again,
and once removed again,
and so on, endlessly.

The plane fact is:
through infinity and eternity
we just change place.

. . .

One thing sure, *"Change!"*
One thing sure, *"No change!"*

RELATIONSHIPS 8/67

Perspective is meaningful
only in relationship to point of view.

Like, what is an ant?
A little bug?

Ha! Little you know!
To a germ, he's a giant.

To a worm,
a scary little animal who suddenly runs over your skin with scratchy feet. *(You would scrunch up your skin and go "OOOZHooHiooooo!")*

Say,
like,
what is an alligator?

I'll tell you!
To us,
he'll bite off your leg!
To happy little fishes
just swimming around in the hot water,
he's a big-daddy
lying in the swamp,
seaweed on his head, over one eye,
sleeping and blinking
and letting flies
light on his nose
without biting them.

But!
What about stars?
Those little lights
high in the sky
at night,
with no clouds
or fog,
(glasses on)
what about them?
What makes them meaningful?
　　　.......
I think, ...
(reflecting-like)
it's because they twinkle
and go 'round and 'round the earth
throughout the ages
and never come down.

VACATION *8/67*

Green leaves, trees and summer air.
Golden girls against the sand, so fair.
And sails are painted on the sea,
motionless beneath the sun.

I drift.
I dream.
I fall asleep and wake,
then fall asleep again.

Slipping gently
through the doors
to sympathetic darkness
and sweet dreams.

The sand is warm,
and far away
my good work lies.
My family, too,
and I am here
with drifting thoughts
and not a single thing to do.

OLEANDERS *8/67*

Somberly I take the air
along macadam pathways in the park,
intent upon my loneliness.
Presently I sit and stare
at Oleander leaves
lightly playing on the air.
How slim their shape.
Like arrowheads in green and black,
and then a burst!
The whitest flower, white!
And then another and another,
'til optimistic, eyes afloat,
I drift right through
and recognize beyond,
in silhouette,
a girl in yellow print.
Lithe,
a third my age,
contemplates a handsome lad,
discusses private things,
sharing,
intent,
until, decisions made,
moves away,
and these old eyes,
relaxed, revived,
return through Oleander leaves
and flowers, white,
to settle down to loneliness again,
lonelier still,
yet strangely mixed with hope.

PURIFICATION *8/67*

*A*scending lithely,
green and firm,
the stem spirals toward the leaf,
which, lying open-faced
and motionless,
drinks the golden rays,
undistracted,
and emanates oxygen,
silently, invisibly,
to sustain our life.

NOT THE EVERYDAY NEWS *8/67*

*N*ot the everyday news!
Please, God,
not today!
I implore,
not think about the war.
Of those who fight,
lose their sight.
Think of all the children,
those who've not reached six,
comprehending commentator's
cultured observations,
reacting to significance
and not to *"tone of voice."*
Disillusionment descending,

more than they could bear,
(We're all to die,
so quick,
so young ....)
and more than I can bear!
Please, God,
I implore,
not today!
Not the everyday news!

PARTICLE OF STAIN *8/67*

*P*articularly formulated
penetrating agent
and a particle of stain
      sinks
        down
          deep.
Absorbed by every fiber on the way.
'til character of wood
and character of stain
are non-existent, vanished,
into something else again.
Something solid to resist
the ever-changing sequences
of wetting-drying,
cold and heat.
An *"Inseparable Team"*
now united, strong as three.
Let the forces disagree!

SOUND WAVES

Sound waves in the air
unheard
to receivers far away.

Music!
Drama!
News!

Flashing round my head.
They bounce,
ricochet,
reflect,
from mountaintops and steeples,
some deflected into space,
ne'er to be heard again.

I walk along
in tall green grass
beneath a purple sky
with just my thoughts
and all those other thoughts
around me
whizzing by.

DO IT NOW *10/67*

*T*o those of you who think you're not
happy in your ignorance, apathetic, comfortable, serene,
    surrounded by the deepest green.
To those of you who shake your heads
    and hearing nothing,
    think your solid cranium
    filled with brains
    instead of merely viscous stuff
    like motor oil or honey,
    let me drop this thought.

See how slowly through it sinks.

Should it ever strike the bottom,
    as it touches,
    just so lightly,
    music, golden,
    brilliant rays,
    illuminate the cavity,
and then you know!

Open wide and sing!
Break right through and past your *"little"* voice!
Break right through to confidence,
    clarity,
    understanding,
    opportunity!

Then do,
before you die!
Sell it all!
Dump it quick on those around you, unenlightened!
Greedily, they'll take your junk.

Then use your newfound gain
to make the image of your newfound self
in three dimensions,
permanent,
concrete,
kick-able,

'ere you're but a whisper.

WELCOME THOUGHT *10/67*

Deep within us, lying clear,
our quiet selves awaits the thought:

*Living by the second,
seldom are we threatened.*

And so our calm selves,
glistening deep,
resolves our doubts,
our tensions, fears,
as the harried raindrop,
swiftly falling,
strikes a waiting lake
and instantly absorbed,
becomes at once,
the whole.

EXPLANATION

*I*n Los Angeles County,
land of the smog,
two hundred thousand kittens each year
are brought to the pound and gassed.

Is there a God?
A rattlesnake I knew
lived a fruitful life,
fathered 80 little ones
without a single wife.

God in action!
Sequence of a Mayfly's dance
is held within the day,
and we expect our 70 years
and don't have much to say.

Where are you, God?
Did I hear you correctly?
You're all of these?
I thought them forces of nature.
One and the same?
Oh! I see.
Yes, that explains it!

THE BUTTERFLY   *10/67*

*O*range and black,
wings outstretched,
the butterfly came gliding by.
Not the flutter type of fly,
but the gliding kind
who only flutters now and then
to keep himself aloft.
Sail, flutter.
Sail, flutter.
I watched him. *(speaker pause)*
He descended all the while,
which made me think
his flutter not enough
to keep him on a level plane,
or something else not quite right.
I just don't know.
Perhaps he bucked a downward draft,
or else a left-ish wing,
tilted out of line,
forced the swooping path,
and he, in desperation, anguish,
fought himself, determined, to the ground.
Or it is quite logical
he just wanted to come down.
Perhaps a flower caught his eye,
or a female butterfly.
At any rate,
before his crash,
I think I saw a furrowed brow
and feelers take a jagged shape,
as straight away
he yawed, skidded, plunged,
into the leafy lawn,

leaving trails of crooked grass
bent almost
to the breaking point.
He struggled up a little dazed,
wobbled to the nearest leaf,
whereon, he gathered wits,
focused eyes,
(Actually quite a job since butterfly's have about 4000.)
and saw before him finally,
his lovely counterpart,
demurely smiling,
obviously thrilled
to see this handsome lad.
And soon with grace,
as only butterflies attain,
they leapt together from the leaf,
and fluttered round about each other,
over the hill and out of sight
of things like you and me
who contemplate things like this.

SOUND OF LIFE *12/67*

*B*eyond my window,
open there,
a fine contralto,
voice in tune,
caught the magic edge of sound,
and with an ever surer grasp,
swelled to her potential,
solid, lasting, musical,

then tapering, full and round,
mellowed on a softer note,
clean and quiet
to the end,
then definitely off.

And so my life,
responding ever stronger
to the steady pull of fate,
runs quickly to the statement,
full and rich,
and then must level off,
quietly fade away.

And egotistically, I hope
that someone close to me,
(when I am gone)
will hear my note
softly on the wind,
and remember me with love.

THE SEARCH *12/67*

*F*or those deficient naturally,
there's nothing but the search.
We read and think and ask ourselves,
and analyze the church.

Aha! You say, just stop the search
and then you'll see,
you'll have it just like me.

The easy sun will warm your toes,
and life will love you as it goes.
I have, at times, stopped the search
and, true, found something there.

Unhappiness in jester's clothes
and staring back with vapid eye.
A blissful world of ignorance
and not a reason why.

There is no doubt,
it's not for me.
Unknowingly, I sigh.

For peace of mind for those unblessed,
the search is grateful, needed rest.

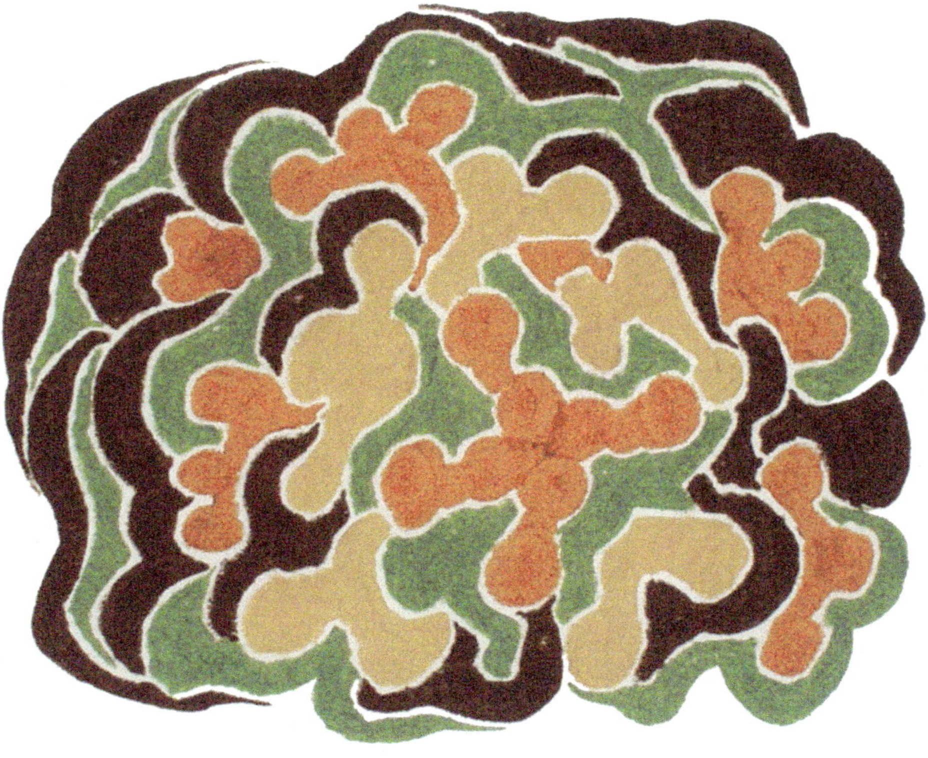

Four

THE AWAKENING *4/73*

Awareness flickered faintly
in the dark behind his eyes
before they opened greatly,
to the wonder of the skies.

For the clouds were slowly lifting
and a vision to behold
with the morning sun behind them
and their edges flaming gold.

And long he lay transfixed
absorbing visually there,
for this, his first experience,
was so wondrously rare.

When swift a rush of wind
descended light upon his ears
and sound became a vital part
of all his tender years.

And raptly did he listen
to the variable breeze
as it hissed along the grasses
and it moaned between the trees.

And wonderment of sight and sound
lay rich within his breast
and he exulted in this being
and was singularly blessed.

When soft along the meadow
wafting sensuous perfumes,
rose a languid winding airway
from the white narcissus blooms

that played about his hair and face
and lingered in his nose
and swept along the length of him
before it gently rose.

And the consciousness of scent arrived
and took it's rightful place,
a third and mighty tool to serve
in loyalty and grace.

And teeming was his mind afraid
to understand his being,
this formidable triumvirate
of scent and sound and seeing.

But as his comprehension
was beginning to improve,
there stirred within his body
a compulsiveness to move,

and blood was full upon his arms
and strength of leg infused,
and neck and chest were charged and taught
and ready to be used.

And lightly did he lift himself
and stood himself erect,
and nostrils flaring, breathed the air
and savored its affect.

FOREST THOUGHTS 6/73
(Exercise in poem writing.)

In a rank and darkened forest
where the eons in their passing
marked the winding pathways
through eternity and night.

Where the tangled fallen oak trees
lay majestic and foreboding
in the veiled and humid dimness
of the early morning light.

And eerie colored night flowers bloom
in gold and green and white,
and blackened silhouettes of leaves
augment the magic sight.

Where insect creatures nightly go
with luminescent eyes,
and only leaves and rotted roots
can hear their mournful cries.

And through the treetops ragged leaves,
against the midnight sky,
a brilliant moon, by Venus chased,
astounds the mortal eye.

Where in the trees a languid breeze
its magic pattern weaves
to stir the latent souls of plants
and rustle all the leaves.

And through the crystal rivulets
the stones like jewels play
and minnows 'gainst the flowing stream
exuberantly play.

Where steady rains come slanting
from a gray and dismal sky
and distant thunder rumbles
to the rain-bird's buoyant cry.

Or evil rains from hurricanes
come stinging in the night
and lightning wracks the universe
in horrid shades of light.

Or drizzle days the forest bathes
in every shade of gray
surrounding every sated leaf,
it smothers out the day.

Where between the hoary roots
the white narcissus blooms
beguiling all the tender night
with sensuous perfumes.

And lichen covered boulder tops
projecting from the ground
observe the microscopic day
an utter not a sound.

Where silence infiltrates the gloom
possessing every leaf,
and violets endure the night
in quiet disbelief.

And not a single creature stirs
or dares to make a sound,
but waits in darkness for the sun
to make its apathetic round.

Where poised upon a silver leaf
a diamond dewdrop glows
and from its luminescent heart
a cosmic power flows.

Beneath some sweeping branch
the sun is flaming high,
the wind and leaves contrive a dance
to mystify the eye.

And north wind swoops and terrifies
the lofty tops of trees,
while fresh and cool beneath the roar
an intermittent breeze.

JOHN HENRY *1/76*

The clear, cool slicing
of a knowing eye.
The growing trust.
Oh, for an idea.
To murk along in the sea
beneath the brown waters,
and think that above the glimmering surface,
the sky, clouds, breeze,
could sweep him into arms of angels.

But there he is, stuck.
Pinned and wriggling,
squirming like a rat
impaled on a prong.
And yet, he knows it's there.
He feels its call, its urgency,
its all life.

Four

But his every effort
mires his being more deeply.
You know, I know, everyone knows, but John,
to live is to let go.

To stop the struggle means an upward float.
With great strength and stillness of will,
he ceases to struggle and slowly, meekly,
gently, rises toward the surface,
the surface and the idea.

Toward the bright light rising,
effortlessly rising,
like a blowfish, brown and prickly,
like a lovely toad ascending
through the muck.

Like a painted eye with a willingness to open,
he lifts and rises, quiescent, still,
will gently nudge the surface,
and there, as if to see the face of God,
will dare to look.

From the lethargy of life withdrawn.
From the gnawing apathy he comes
to nudge the surface of the light,
the mind, the vision,
the idea.

At the surface, face to face,
and looking only lightly,
for eagerness would blinding be,
destroying his ability,
to perceive.

And so it passed,
John Henry slowly merged
with flowing grains and window panes
and sunlight on a smiling house
and children's laughter in the wind.

He came to merge
with the living presence,
from the tepid sea arisen,
by welcome strangers hand's uplifted,
came to look at you and me.

UNTIMELY WIND 1/76

*U*nconfined,
the hot, untimely wind
is whistling through the canyons,
roaring through the trees,
combing the dry grasses
and brittle chaparral.

Unheededly,
she drives,
compulsive and abandoned,
toward the sea.
I feel her strength,
her utter freedom,
as she sweeps toward the sea.
She must pay an urgent visit
to the surface of the sea.

Unconfined,
the hot, untimely wind
comes whispering, moaning,
comes crying through the grasses,
the blackened chaparral.

Unheedfully,
she's going.
Abandoned,
she's flowing
to the sea.

She bows her head
and pressures
toward the sea.

WHERE WILL I GO? *1/76*

*H*ow am I love?
By lust and here.
What will I can?
What I do, I do.
Where will I death?
Will go, will go.

THE ANT AND GOD

I see the ant.
I step over him.
He sees me not,
nor my typewriter,
which I carry.
He hurries,
steadfast,
on his way.

I know God
as the ant knows me,
and my typewriter.

EXTRAS

Similarity

A tree has a root.
I have a foot.

Poison Oak

*P*oison Oak is rich
in itch.

Both Exhumed

The infinite gloom
of a forgotten room.
Dead in mother's womb.
A Pharaoh's tomb.
Both exhumed.

Hate

Hate is death
with every breath.

Grass

Tall grass listens
while it glistens.

Rollo's Directions

To stare at a ceiling
and drum up a feeling
is very rough, indeed.

But if you follow
the directions of Rollo,
you'll get some kind of lead.

To get an emotion
you put on a lotion
and peck at a handful of seed.

Flowers

Crowds of flowers
smile for hours.

Wife

A wife arising
is surprising.

Poetic Thought

The poetic thought
is heavily wrought
with thinking
and mild reverie.
And things I think
can never be thought,
can never be bought,
but must be thought by me.

Going Fast

Freedom is thinking you're free.
Loving is loving to be.
Dying occurs at the last.
The first two really go fast.

Blueberry Sot

The branberry pot
was certainly hot.
Who couldn't care less was me.
The blueberry sot
asleep on the cot
was under the branberry tree.

Tree in Rain

During the momentary,
the Oak tree,
lashing
curled its roots
and scrabbling
for a better grip,
ferocity
closed its eyes
of the noon-day
bowed its head,
blustering
hugged its body
rainstorm
with its branches.

NOT POLITE

At the speed of light
times ten,
the star moves away from me.
Where is it going?
Why so fast?
Why does it go at all?
It should be content
to remain in place
and behave,
that I may study it,
take notes,
exhaust it's secrets.
I'm not used to
things retreating,
things so big,
things so bright,
things ferocious in the night.
A star should stick around,
keep me company,
advise me when I'm sick,
entertain me when I'm well.
I should take a star for granted,
but it won't let me.
Insists on blazing away
at the speed of light,
times ten,
burning with the audacity of a million suns,
going to places I'd never go.
Rocketing away
through a frozen night,
not looking back,
not thinking of me,
not polite.

COSMIC CLOCK 2/76

*I*n a single tick
of the Cosmic Clock,
I am strata.

BIRTH 2/76

*S*till – stillness
breathlessly waiting
space unfilled
purposefully seeded
a resting and freshness.

A stillness of snow
drifted and sloping
a silent glazed surface
a hoping.

A cross-threaded web
moves on the wind
silent and floating
awaiting.

Shell in a sandstone
locked in the darkness
endlessly waiting
forbearing.

A waiting and breathing
silent and living
a purposeful waiting
fulfilling.

A stillness and blackness
a warm moonless night
a soft wind awafting
a stirring.

Time is for waiting
deciduous tree
content with it's juices
abiding.

Compulsively beating
a beating with meaning
things in brown mud
wait for a bursting.

A mild agitation
fluid-like motion
disturbingly strong
fascination.

Wind in the willows
rising at night
freshens the leaves
delighting.

Discomfort and beating
warm and unseeing
a floating and twisting
and coming to rest.

Earth's giant cycles
creating the seasons
a cooling and warming
never to rest.

A pressure releasing
warmness and weary
progressively urgent
repeating and beating,
anxious, retreating.
A squeezing and helplessness
a blazing white light
a freezing white nightmare
a flailing at night
a drowning in sound
a screaming!

ANOTHER DAY *2/76*

*A*nd so you say
you won't come in,
and I wanting you so
to stay and talk to me,
you refuse with,
"Really, I must go.
This splitting headache
hurts me so."
And I, wanting not to hurt your feelings, reply,
"Oh, my poor dear kitten,
may I get you something?"

And then you say,
"Really, no. I must be going.
Thank you for everything.
You've been so kind.
Please, do not walk me to the car.
I shall be fine."
"When will I see you?"
Say I, blurting it out,
looking you in the eyes,
those eyes that once shone so bright
with laughter and life,
now with a tear
just in the corner
and little crinkle lines
of life's concerns.
"Another day," she says
and walks away.
I follow her with my eyes.
Her comely shape,
her corseted thigh,
her white gloved hands
and Sunday hat
held with a pin
and one gray hair,
drifting, astray,
on the wind.
The sound of a motor car driving off.
And then she is gone.
Silence strikes me, sudden,
as a fall in the night.
I fall into reverie
and memory,
of all the things
she'd meant to me
and all the things
I'd meant to be.

And so,
perhaps it's better this way.
"Another day." she'd said.
Perhaps, again, I say,
"Another day."
I turn and walk back in.

I ROLL A ROCK 2/76

I roll a rock
that would roll on me.
I will prevail,
eventually.

MODERATION 2/76

I am not my name.
I am not what I've done.
I am not what I think I'll do.

By the time I say
I am,
I am not.

*I walk through space
and step through faith.*

I am a process
always in motion,
my grave my destination.

SOMEBODY ELSE   2/76

The real me
is somebody else.

EMANUEL   2/76

EMANUEL!
Where are you?
Leaping from a cloud,
tiny stick-figure,
smaller than the sun,
gleefully falling,
arms awry,
into another billowy bed?
You're not dead!

EMANUEL!
Come out now.
I see you there,

seaweed in your hair,
playing with seashells
and patterns of sunlight
on jewel-strewn sand
in a salt water land.

*E*MANUEL!
Is that you
that I barely see,
through swamp mist,
drifting, silvery,
atop the cypress tree,
beckoning me?

*E*MANUEL!
Please talk to me.
You with eyes
that see through mine.
You, whose soul
knows all souls.
You, with time
that knows no time.
Tell me I belong to you.
Tell me you love me, too.
Show me again
the variety and range
of what I long to do.

TIME IS A PLACE

*T*ime is a place.
Eyes open.
Eyes closed.

Quickly I capture
the place where I was,
never to see it again.

Eyes of the near-dead
lost in the past.
Eyes of a lover
conceding at last.
Eyes in the mirror
thoughtfully cast.

A click of the clock
and the world makes a change,
and no way on earth to stop.

Eyes closed,
eyes open,
eyes closed.

Quickly I capture
the place where I was,
never to be it again.

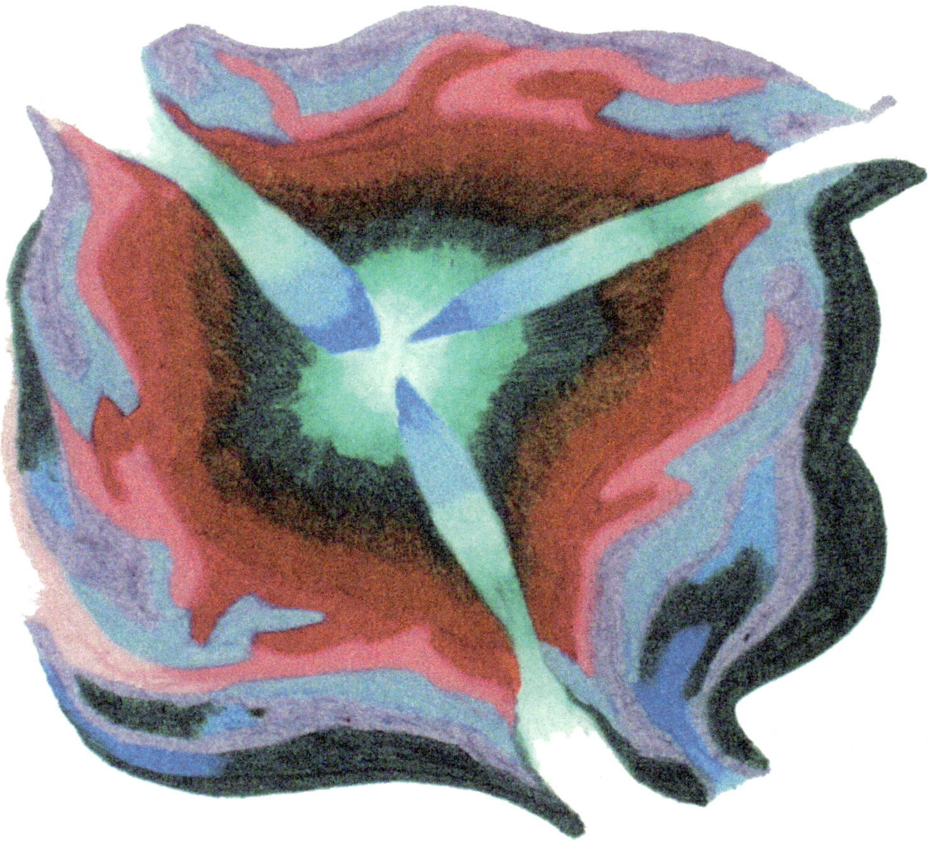

Five

WHERE ARE YOU, JOHN? *2/76*

"Where are you, John?"
asked Phyllis.

Nine fine planets,
earth and moon,
singing along
on a silver thread,
winging along
through the frozen void
of an airless night
to the end of time
at the speed of light,

and as they travel,
they orbit the sun,
and as they orbit,
they rotate.

"I'm here, Phyllis."
cried John.

THE UNIVERSE I SEE *2/76*

When the moon comes up
behind the hard-edged mountain,
I see my massive planet in rotation.
It strikes me again,
I cling to a ball
that hurtles through nothingness
toward nothing at all.
It saddens me to be rushing,
insignificant, small,
on my way,
to places I'll never see,
clinging to a ball.

And then,
because futility is not a pleasant state,
I console myself,
that, at least,
my planet was made for me.
It contains a beauty
I alone can see.

The stars are never dull,
but shine with life intensely,
as I do too.
And things down here
are arranged for me,
like silver clouds
and friendly crowds,
my lively friends,
the birds and bees,
my maltese,
and all they do,
and all I do.

I vow to make the best of it
by being what I am;
what I was meant to be.

Think!

I may be a giant universe,
myself,
to some bright mite.
It's then I know I'm worth it,
really big,
like a planet,
like a sun.
It's then I know
that all that whirling,
burning, universes I contain,
make something I call me.

You might say
that I'm the end result
of all that speeding.
You might say
that futile flight
of all the starry universe

is going straight to me.
I'm the nowhere planets go.

The universe is me.

THE END RESULT   2/76

*I*t pleases me to know
the galaxies I see
*(and those I don't,
but know through scientist's
work in astronomy)*
may have an end result
much like me.

The stars are minute parts
of some immense being,
just like me,
and all the endless
exploding, rotating,
orbiting, clustering,
gaseous, super-dense
matter out there,
derive their meaning
from the act of being
the vital parts
of a thing like me.

Incomprehensible
and huge am I
to other living things,

like germs and cells
that dwell within me.

If I were a cell,
couldn't I see
atoms, electrons,
as fleeing stars
of which I'm the whole,
speeding away
through a frozen night,
destination: nowhere,
furious, bright.

And so, I believe
that I'm a universe
because my existence,
like the stars I see,
is incomprehensible
to parts of me.

I'm the result
of immense energy.
I'm the result
of the stars I see.

CONSIDER THIS 2/76

Consider this:
A star can't think
or talk or feel.
A satellite can't fight.

The moon can never hum a tune,
but only reflects light.
A galaxy can never see
or drink a cup of tea.
I think I've got a universe
for little you and me.

LET'S STAY HOME 2/76

The Milky Way
is in the way.
The universe can't cook.
The black hole
has no soul.
Let's stay home and look.

The sun doesn't know
how roses grow.
The moon is a goon with a light.
The temperature's nifty
below seven-fifty,
Let's stay home and write.

Saturns's rings,
really stings.
A satellite's a sight.
And noxious gasses
will cover your glasses.
Let's stay home tonight.

GROWTH OF UNIVERSES

*S*oft are raindrops
surprising leaves
lifted in prayer
from sinewy stems
laden with sap,
virally twisted,
secure in groups,
radiate light,
bright,
life.

While massive,
through deep water,
a coasting whale
slips through darkness,
silent,
vast,
encrusted with lifetimes.

Softly the raindrops
surprising leaves,
slathering skins,
and slaking thirst
encourage growth
of the universe.

FISH WITH A WISH 2/76

For a million years
I have lived in the sea.
I have eaten a billion other fish
to survive.
I have escaped a million fish
who would have eaten me.
My species is in jeopardy.
I know what it is
that I must do
to stay alive.
I know what nature
will have me do
to survive.
And so I find myself
cast on shore
a fish
with a wish
to stay alive.

WHAT I DID NOT FIND 3/76

I heard nothing under a bush
but my own ears ringing.
I saw patterns against the sky
in infinite variety.
They were surprised when they saw me,
but did not cast me out.

I rest.

The various patterns move in the sky,
delighting my eye.
Who am I that sees?
Who am I that occupies
this strange shape,
eyes that see,
mind and body.
Electricity flows.
I function.
It's obvious I'm made
to go anywhere,
do anything.
But going and doing
must be decided
somewhere inside
by someone that's known as me.
Decisions! Decisions!

I sleep.

Click goes the clock – another notch.
The earth continues to spin.
I am older.
Nothing remains the sa ...
I'm rudely awakened!

SLEEP *3/76*

*O*n hands and knees
I creep

through a field
of foolish yellow daisies.

Wild of eye,
they gesture,
oblivious to night,
in fading light.

Eventually,
I sleep
beneath the stars.

EXTRAS *3/76*

Stopped by glass

The rain tries to reach me.
Stopped by glass!
Breezes try to teach me.
Stopped by glass!
Birds would like to sing to me.
Stopped by glass!
Bells would like to ring to me.
Stopped by glass!
Guess I'll go outside.

Poor Passerby

The leaves, dirt, cinders
tumbled by
blackening the passerby.

Nonsense

The rain that strikes my window pane
and following down the glass
to mingle with the flowers
and the flowing grass
can kiss my ass.

More Nonsense

Down the lanes of window panes.
In the store for more.
Down the chute came a boot.
From the shore, the roar.

Immaculate

Immaculate
the hearts of angels.
We have time.
Purely sings the winds of ages.
And so is mine.

Geronimo Quoir

The Geronimo Quoir
conducted by Doug Rucker
will now sing the beautiful
Brahms Wreckwiam.

Ants

a   *"You have ants!"*

b   *"They're not mine."*

Sun

*T*he dazzling sun
shrivels the day
as a leaf that curls
and blackening,
burns and blows away.

ON THE RAGGED EDGE 3/76

*O*n the ragged edge
I hold with bleeding nails,
waiting for a change,
from within
or without.
On a razors edge, I balance,
no shoes, no umbrella.
Were I to stand still,
then should I be sliced through
as an orange upon a block,
quivering in halves,
double dead.
Perhaps the teeth of gears will snap.
Perhaps a flood will wash us all away.
Perhaps the sun will burn us black.
I wait for the day.

BONY-RIDGE *3/76*

*I*n the starry, faint light of predawn,
nine of us lifting, step on strong step,
into the bowers of sagebrush and grease-wood,
the warmth of our bodies working and beating,
we moved with our heartbeats
into the climb.

An hour sped as the stars,
the cool perspiration attending our brows,
when rounding a tree silhouette in the sky,
and freshness and coolness descending,
we came to a viewing place, heart's desire.

High on the side of the black-caverned mountain,
with Bony-Ridge, massive, looming behind,
and mysterious velvety dark plains below,
high on a promontory, boldly projecting,
with grease-wood and boulders thrusting, awry,
we settled ourselves in our collars and waited.

The sound of the wind and the wind on my face,
a powerful ebbing and flowing with grace,
she whispered to sagebrush and thick chaparral,
and moistened my eyes, and bid me well.

Our senses thus tuned to the stirrings of nature,
in the lightening darkness, we crouched in the coolness,
our hands in our pockets, for our friend we waited,
awaiting the rise of the sun.

Everyone heard them first.
The birds, with music, awakening the day.
The calling, the chattering, the musical phrases,

came straight from their hearts.
No coaxing or redness of faces.
No shyness or lowering of heads.
No pounding of hearts or prompting,
but straight from their being they sang.
Today I would be like the birds.

I do not know when the stars went away,
or when the comet faded from view.
I do not know when the blackness of sky
changed from deep purple to blue.
But slowly and softly the process of changing
included me, too.

Intent on my listening to birds and the wind.
Intent on the landscape below, now revealing,
Intent on the bouldery grayness around me,
those boulders all pock-marked by passings of eons,
the rainstorms and windstorms and sunlight prevailing,
the knowledge of life-forms in growing and passing,
intent on my being, I waited.

The velvet green landscape below,
the mountainous spines hard-lining the sky,
the boulders compliantly thrusting,
were fused into one,
and the dark of my body and soul,
and the dark of the mountainous landscape around me,
gradually lightened, gradually, brightened,
moving toward a whole.

Then in soft light of pre-dawning,
the steady flow of the wind still sighing,
the youngest of us, a golden-haired girl,
danced with a Toyon as it moved in the wind.
Danced with her delicate arms now swaying.
Danced with her torso, now stiffly bending,

Five 103

as the limbs of the brush resisted the wind,
and her hands flowed with the fluttering leaves,
and fingers, so pliant and willing, echoed the rhythms.
And the strong wind, cold on her skin, encouraged them both.
The sensitive girl,
warm blood resisting, and one with her partner,
were dancing as though they had always been dancing.
They danced while awaiting the day.

Before the sun has burst on the land.
Just a moment before that moment of triumph.
The time when Mother-Sun brightens the sky,
revealing the mystery of the pre-dawn land,
when the flowing landscape, rich green-gray,
strung together with soot-black shadows,
when patterns a thousand feet below
divide themselves into curving and curious shapes,
when birds are blending into the richest variety,
and the strong wind, restrained,
pushes past to round the earth,
the chaparral responding and stiffly wavering,
and though she's not revealed herself,
the Sun,
strong mother of all we know,
about to stun the world,
to reveal herself with the power of fire,
and the infinite beauty born of her body,
and darkening, even yet, that ridge dividing,
behind which she has chosen to rise,
as if to make emerging even more astounding,
the ridge, the dividing line,
light as all light, above,
dark as the night, below,
we, nine, stand close.

Feeling the warmth and the presence of all,
hearing the songs and the sounds of the earth,

and watching, intently, the place of the rising,
we see the first ray.

And the circles of light begin their rotation.
Tiny circles of light flowing clockwise and back.
I dare not see the edge of the sun,
so piercingly, gloriously, bright are her rays.

She has me!

I am hers.
She claims us for another day.
Her shafts are boundless.
She exposes the valleys and shadows below us.
Behind us the ancient and looming rocks all aglow,
on fire, pink and gray.
Even the wind recedes in deference.
The birds do not recede in their singing.
nor do we, for our hearts are brimming.

Now the bouldery, pock-marked ridge
swells with pride and meaning.
It drinks in the light and the strength of the sun,
and thus, energy infused, radiates heat.
And the color and shadow and intensity reflects upon us.
Our faces are beaming,
and the circles of light, quietly circling,
and the earth in its rotation,
and the landscape below.

GO FIND YOURSELF

3/76

*G*o find yourself was the word.
Mingle with nature and soak up her soul.
Blend with the landscape as the bird and the deer.
Find what it means to not be yourself.
See what it's like to be part, not the whole.
Time not to be your name.
Time not to be your past.
Time not to do what's expected.
Expect *nothing* of you,
but see how you flow.
See where you'll go.
Find what you know.

THE CAVES

3/76

"Find the caves." she said.
I marched on a path so long,
I'd despaired of its end.
I followed a glorious canyon
with clear, shear walls.
There, across the void,
circling hawks or crows,
or turkey buzzards, ten or twenty,
rotating high.
Their shadows zip up,
down, across
the vertical canyon wall

in crazy directions, patterns,
as they come closer to,
or farther from
the flat stone cliff.
Some dead thing, no doubt.
I hope it's not a traveler.
Perhaps and old Indian.
Chumash?

I came to a boulder marked *"echo,"*
but I did not try.

I saw the teetering rock,
bottom up, on its point.
Would I be awed, should I see it fall
to a shattering death on the canyon floor.

What's this?
A beautiful top
of a massive rock,
jutting precariously.
Gingerly, I climb out.
The sun is hot.
I am sleepy.
I fling my arms wide to the side,
and settle myself in a careless sprawl,
in the stillness of the air,
in the hotness of the sun,
in the dangerousness of my resting place,
I relax,
and drift away.

Sometime later
a cooler breeze
from the canyon trees
begins to go.
I try to ignore it.

I turn my back to it.
I let it blow.
Nevertheless,
it's persistently cold.
I move away among the twigs
and ants and branches
half beneath a sagebrush.
There, hat over eyes,
I continue a fitful nap.
Presently, I'm found.
We two, hike on back.

MEETING PLACE   *3/76*

Trudging back, I fall behind.
So does my friend.
We talk of how and what to paint.
We talk of death and life and birth.
We exchange emotions, ideas and notions.
We find our similar values.
We ignore our dissimilar ones.
Wagging our tails, we enjoy the day.

No one selected the meeting place.
Two were resting,
three came soon,
and two were last.
Listen to the tired banter,
free and from the heart.
Stories, ribbing,
jokes, ad-libbing,

sitting or lying,
nibbling or sighing,
we gather strength
for the great descent.

Into a common fabric
our personalities we weave,
then, as a group, we arise
and leave.

SHORTED OUT 3/76

100 watt bulb,
300 watt jolt.

Trembling, I wait
under the lightning bolt.
300 amp jolt,
100 amp capacity.

I hiss and spark,
(a waning tenacity)

and flare and smoke.
In the dim-damp-dark,
I rattle my wires
and dance on rocks,
set electric fires.

A low-voltage box,
overloaded
by incoming current.

Exploded, no doubt
by overwork, goaded,

shorted out!

LOST SON 3/76

I say to the boy,
"How are you, boy?"
He looks at me
with open eyes
as if to ask,
"Who are you?
and,
"Why do you wish to know?"
I smile an easy smile,
take off my hat,
and with handkerchief
so slightly soiled,
I wipe my brow.
Uneasily, I say,

"You are my own,
the one I love,
the boy I've kept
as part of me
for, lo, these years.
The one I've longed to hold
so close within my arms
until the days and hours
of all the time

whereof we've lost
shall come to catch us
once again
and we are filled to overflowing,
with love, glowing."

He looks to his shoes,
hands shoved in pockets,
shoulders hunched,
says to my face,
"Are you nuts?"

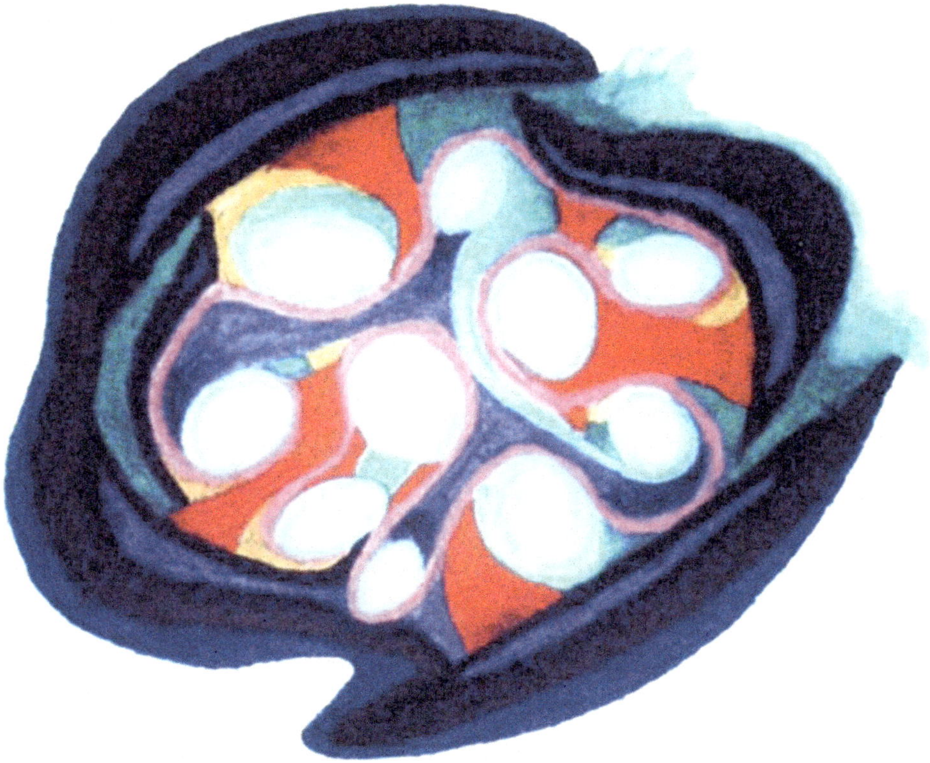

Six

WHAT DO YOU SEE? 3/76

Now that we are alone
and you have shown me
that you like me
and you trust me,
please, sit with me
and let us be together.
...

Pleasant, isn't it?
Just you and I
and the setting sun
about to sink beneath the sea?

Breathe deeply the twilight air
and as the sun's last rays
are just a moment gone,
exhale,
and as you do,
imagine your eyes,
still closed,
on a vertical axis,
turning,
in whichever direction you like,
slowly at first,
in perfect unison,
twirling.
That's right.
Relaxed and alert,
let your eyes in their
whirling
pick up speed.
...
And now
they are rapidly spinning,
silently spinning
behind your lids.

Whirling in unison,
perfectly matched,
steady as lead.
Let them spin
for a moment or two.
...
Enjoy it.
...

And now they are slowing.
More slowly they spin.
Silently rotating,

ever more slowly.
...

Now they are turning,
as in the beginning,
hardly at all.
Relaxed and alert,
...
Enjoy it.
...
When I give the signal to stop
your eyes will click to a stop,
however, instead of you facing them out to the world,
they will come to a stop
facing in,
into your center,
into the heart and the soul of your being.

STOP!

What do you see?

I see a blackened void
endless in dimension
where nothing will reside.

From my inward looking eyes,
stationary,
unmoving in the darkness,
I step,
as a tiny man,
to explore the immense dark cavern.
Unafraid, I go hunting
with my candle
through the blackness
and the vastness
of the void.

I know there is a something,
some dark secret

somewhere lurking
on the edges of the room.
What's this?

A room of many brown faced doors,
on the walls, floor, ceiling,
each with jeweled handle thrusting,
inviting me to open.

I try the first.
A shaft of light so blinding
strikes me full upon the face.
It makes me squint,
and then the misty whiteness
of a lonely beach
and fog in wisps and clearing,
sunlight penetrating
to the rippling sand.
I see the frothy tongues
of muted waves
come licking at my toes
and biting me with cold
and in the distance,
out to sea,
I hear a joyful singing
and then the somber ringing
of a low-pitched bell,
struck in perfect measured time,
and the singing and the bell
in utter contrast mingling.
The song,
a sound of sweetness,
love and joy in living.
The bell,
a doleful measuring
of time going by.

I close the door,
reflecting,
and in a moment,
curious again,
grasp another jeweled handle.

Gently, I open
and look directly into eyes
that look directly into mine.
I see the soul of another being
as that other being searches mine.

We smile.
We cry.
We love.
We walk, hand in hand,
into an unlikely land
where a tree is a tree
and a me is a me.
We ask a bird, *"How do you fly?"*
and away on the wind he soars.

We ask the bush,
"How do you grow?"
and a flower springs from the bud.

We ask the stone,
*"Why do you sit,
heavy, still,
in the heat of the desert day?"*
The insect creatures beneath,
stir in the coolness,
awaiting the night.

We lie in the shade
of a pepper grove
on bluffs that fall to the sea,

and watch the billowing clouds
drag their rainstorm feet.

We feel the cooler breeze
descending from the trees.
Inhale the dampened freshness
of the eucalyptus leaves.

We hear the pattering sounds
of raindrops on our palms
and fingertips
and taste the droplets
on our lips,
so content we are to be.

A draft, ominous, cold,
from the open door and black beyond,
shatters my serenity.
I step back,
reluctantly,
through the open door,
and gently let it close.

Back again,.
within the dimness of my mind,
I select another jeweled handle
and pull it once again.

I become disheartened
by a melancholy room
painted black,
yet glowing somber red,
and on a flowered platform
stands an open coffin
and a stiffened human form
lying petrified within.
I close the door
and close my eyes.

Unhappily, within my brain,
the dreadful image
I yet retain.

I look for the entrance eyes
and see them, as before,
staring blankly in.
As a tiny man,
quickly, I climb out
to daylight,
sanity and fresh air.

EXTRAS *4/76*

My Hope

I hope today
to not be me,
valuing, as I do,
anonymity.

Henry, Give Up

*W*hen will Henry give it up?
The lady hasn't gone away.
He handed her the silver cup,
but said she couldn't stay.

Insult

Grass sings tenor,
bushes, base.
Clouds sing alto
in your face.

Whimpering Willow

Whimpering,
the willow
drops her head,
hangs her arms
and sighing,
responds
to breezes,
crying.

Trees

Forest trees,
strong of trunk,
claim their spaces.

At intervals
they grunt
and turn their faces.

BREAK SERENELY ON THE DAY 4/76

The day breaks
serenely.
It is I
who add turmoil
and color it tense.
It doesn't make sense.
I should break serenely
on the day,
however it shows,
whether it blows
or rains,
or bakes,
or snows.
I must learn the way
to break
serenely
on the day

RAIN 4/76

Overhead,
whispering clouds
plan a mischief,
then scatter,
whistling,
to their posts.

What is it
in the rushes?
A rowboat!
Rotted, resting.
Paint-peeled prow
rudely thrusting.
It lies in death.
Moss sucks its marrow.

Lightly laps the water.
Brightly play the minnows.
Tightly grows the seaweed
in the luminescent shade.
A finely textured drizzle falls.
A night bird calls.
And from the trees
a cooler breeze,
then full-blown rain.

RAGGED DAYS 4/76

And then the ragged days
and variety of ways
the Mother Earth will speak.
We will seek to understand the land
and how the windstorm plays
with broken bottles on the sand
and the seagull's beak
and the military band.

I see a mountain peak
and massive rocks
that saw the sky.
I see a cloud that stands on end,
dirigible upended,
sinking through the honeyed air.
I hear an iron bell
tolling out the day
and taste the rain
sticking to my fingertips
with my tongue and lips,
and a white-gloved dowager sips
a sugared lemon drink
on the brink of sanity
and vanity
and boredom
and goredom.

THE SECRETS *4/76*

little do they
in the dark of their own,
knowing what and why,
yet not telling,
or saying,
or stating,
or communicating,
in any way,
but with serious countenance
and intense thought,
even though ordinary,

or strange,
or for that matter,
both, even so,
we knew
and we told them,
but they wouldn't,
or couldn't.
even the will-o-the-wisp,
won't.
they could if they tried,
but they don't.
if they were paid,
they would,
but no-one pays me
or my family tree.
and so I sit,
thinking, rocking,
not blaming
or lauding,
but letting the world,
confiding it's secrets
to nobody else
but you.

WHAT I SEE 4/76

I see seaweed
flowing
and immensely
is it growing
in the shining

silver surface
of the undulating sea.

I see a dove
that rides upon the wind,
way up high,
wings outreaching,
white against the deep blue sky.
The dove, a moving
line of grace,
and a smile
upon my face
begins to form,
for it is warm.

WHAT I SEE (2) 4/76

I see grass
ten feet tall
and animals
that look like ants
disappearing there,
along the walks,
and white mites,
motionless,
upon the stalks,
and blending,
as the blades
are bending,
in the intermittent
breeze.

I see weeds
as tall as trees
with giant leaves
and spreading,
crowned with silver balls
that, shredding,
float upon the wind.

I see roots,
tangled, working,
intertwined
and moving shapes
in shadows, lurking,
indefinite and queer
and, as the light recedes,
it hides misdeeds
of living things
in giant grass.

SURPRISE 4/76

I sing the song
of the sing-a-long
and in every wretched way,
dally away the day.
Until the rise
of the great surprise,
(and none too soon)
the full moon.

I then become serious
instead of delerious
and sleep, the next day,
'til noon.

LATE SUMMER 4/76

I feel the humid atmosphere
clinging to my skin.
I perspire clean water
and breath heavy air.

I sit in my chair
observing bark of trees
and dripping leaves,
low slung clouds
and droplet crowds
clinging to the eaves.

I listen for rumblings
of late summer thunder
and wonder at living things
that gnaw at roots
of long green grass
and baby sucker shoots
naive beneath the sky.
I see violets leaping
on too tall stems,
and ivy tendrils creeping
on the back yard fence.

The vegetable world is dense,
and I dream on these things,
on dragon fly wings,
suppertime laughter,
sleeping dogs,
and what fall brings.

SPIRIT OF MAN   **4/76**

Music descending
from another time,
another age,
than mine.

Spirit of the long-dead,
living now, as then.

Through paper marks,
brain, ears and hand,
I know the man,
and how he lived.

His music speaks to me
of his integrity.

I see fingers,
strong,
like hammers,
sounding on the keys.

He tells me how it is,
and how it was.

I feel the strength and arch
of every finger
as it strikes,
resounding,
on the strings.

I feel the joy
I know he felt
while in his moments,
living,
unaware,
lost in life,
at the center of his being.

Were my life
to have such meaning.

MOONLIGHT SHADOWS   *5/76*

Moonlight,
leaves,
and quivering shadows,
tell a silent tale
on the midnight floor.
If no-one sees,
it speaks,
(the shadow trees)
to inanimate friends
who can't reply
or understand.
Perhaps a moth

will trace a path
from dark to light,
and quiver and merge
with shivering shadows
of stems and leaves,
until it enters the dark once more,
The shadows last chance,
it makes a measured pass
across the floor,
over the spread,
and halfway up the headboard wall,
before dawn arrives
and it evaporates away.

EXTRAS 5/76

Void is Black

The void is black and fearfully made.
The moon spewed from her side.
Sprouting wings, lifts from the sea,
swelling, filling the void, and drifting.
Inwardly walking, infinite, caring.
At peace with herself, at last.
Gliding above the vengeful waves.

Stroboscope

Shot by a stroboscope,
in each bright posture,

in every nuance and gesture,
I'm seen.
I dance in space,
and the flashing light,
in measured time,
catches my life
in angular attitudes.

Shit-fit

*P*it, hit,
snit,
spit,
shit-fit!
The above words,
on a specific night,
when I,
feeling gloomy,
choose to write,
and with nothing to state,
and yet a desire to communicate,
must choose this way
to darken my day.
Please don't be upset.

Mirrored Mind

Alone in the seat
of the mirrored mind
I see myself reflected,
the infinite me,
in all directions,
multiplied.

Repair Job

Caught in sleep's grasp,
I run at half-speed,
ready for full-stop.
How quickly the night
will zip through.
I hope to see the day
in three dimensions, moving,
not just pictures in my mind.
I do need a repair job.
Tonight I shall have it done.

Crackers

I'd like you to meet
my good friend,
James Cracker,
his brother, Graham,
and his lovely wife,
Polly-Wanna.

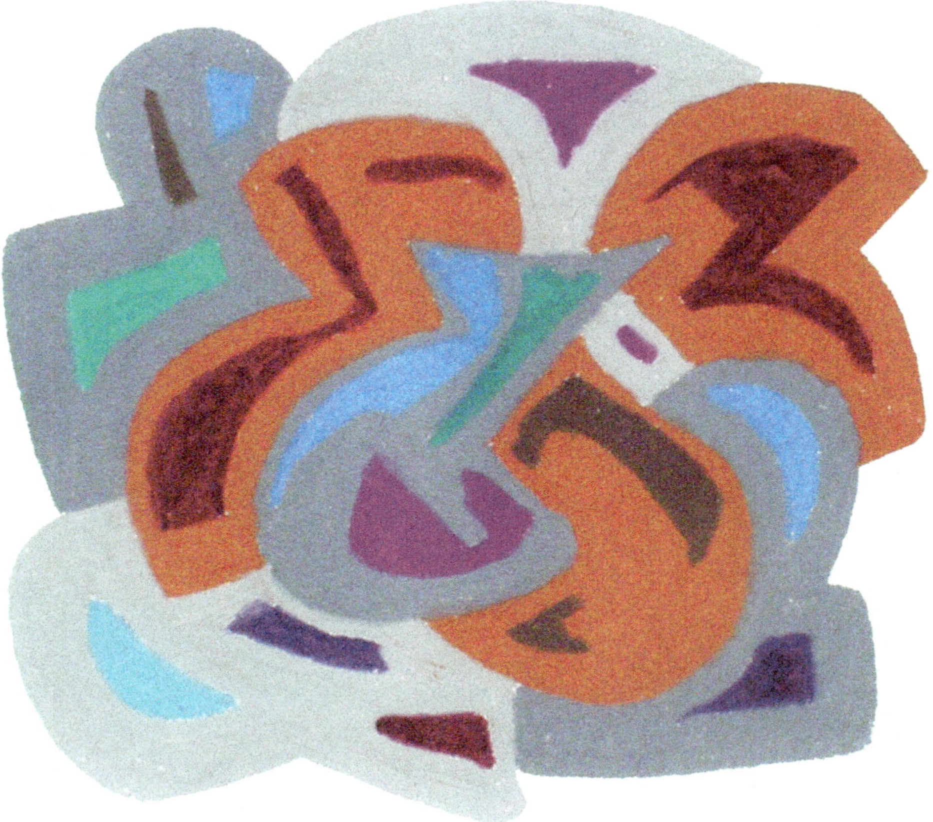

Seven

MORE RAIN 7/76

By an open window,
sleeping, content, smiling,
I sleep on.
By the open window,
I wait for rain.
I know it's coming.
I smile and wait,
warm, snug, protected and content,
having been tucked-in and kissed.
Smiling, I close my eyes and wait for rain.
The wind has been strong,
but now it is still, hushed, expectant,
and then a cooler rush of wind

and thick droplets pad the sill, leaves, grass.
The sound on the roof is bliss.
I relax, warm, snug, kissed and content.
I sleep and the rain spatters the window sill
and onto my smiling face.
I hear thunder rolling through the heavens,
and a lightning flash
brightens the lids of my eyes,
and the rain, renewed, splatters,
ever more sharply on the sill,
and tiny droplets are on my peaceful, sleepy, smiling face.
It rains with a rush, now intense.
The air is thick with raindrops
slanting into the yard, leaves, roof, earth.
The heart of the rain
and the cool wind are upon me now,
and I am secure in my bed,
perfectly sheltered by the close overhead roof
and it's roar
and the gutters are spilling
and rivulets in the grass have formed
and are draining
and I doze and smile
and soon the heavens lighten again
and the thunder booms through the clouds, again,
and I sleep, contented, warm, relaxed,
smiling, kissed, loved and sheltered
through the long night rain.

I AM 8/76

I am.
I hear.
I see.
I feel.
I have energy.
I have latent energy.
My energy waits.
I reign it in.
I do not release it.
I am filled with it
to the brim.
I save it.
My heart beats quietly,
solemnly,
waiting,
powerfully,
capable of delivering
all the I am there is,
soon!

I SHALL BURST 8/76

I am charged and ready to burst.
Like a Fourth of July bomb,
I wait, wick extended,
ready for lighting.
Silently, I walk,
cool air in my nostrils.

My feet are cold,
the stars unusually bright.
I look for Mars.
I do not think,
yet feel my thoughts.
I am.
I wait, discontented.
I'd like to lose myself in running.
Run for a hundred miles
through twilight, night and dawning.
Then, exhausted, I would fall beneath a Sumac,
lost, and sleep an eternity.
My energy is boundless,
yet I do nothing.
I am hostile. I am strong.
I am frustrated. I am belligerent.
My fathomless energy seems futile,
though it is where I live.
I wait for the right time.
Charged and ready,
I wait for the proper moment.
I wait for the gears of the world
and the signs of the earth to adjust.
Then, shall I burst.

THIRD BRAIN DOWN 8/76

Deep in the deep.
Deepest – deeper,
thinking, third brain down.
Thinking deep with feeling.
Feeling deep with thinking.
All of a piece.

Energetic lethargy,
super-concerned
and solid,
like thick, tough meat,
I think-feel,
and feel-think.
I feel what I know,
deeply, deepest
deeper,
third brain down.

I SIT IN BETWEEN   *8/76*

I sit in between
wanting and caring,
hoping to shed some light,
hoping to guide,
    to teach,
    to show the way,
in some slight quandary
ready to speak my mind,
should I find the way,
    the proper time,
    the place.
And what attitude should I assume
and what attitude shall I find.
    Dear children,
    I want more than anything
    for you to take joy
    in being you.

BAOBOB   *8/76*

The Baobob sucks
at the juice of my life.
It has rooted my planet
through lack of attention.
I must dig it out
whatever the cost,
and when it is gone
plant flowers and fruits
and pay more attention.

BODY   *8/76*

Clean cotton shirt.
Clean cotton pants.
Clean body, fine body, lean body,
fits in my clothes.
I lie still, refreshed, and feel good in my body.
I feel nothing but warmth and contentment
as my bright blood flows it's effortless way.
It visits my toes and heart and hands.
I tingle with health.
It feels good to live here.
I love it here.
I wear clean, fine-fitting clothes
of skin, muscles, guts and bones.
I like it here.
I could live here always.

I am at home in my body.
This is where I live,
fully oxygenated with relaxed muscle tone,
not hungry or thirsty or out of breath,
not needing of elimination,
not gurgling or inwardly working,
not gaseous or nauseous
or overeaten of useless foods.
I lie on my bed, a mass of living cells,
meat and bone, with emotions, brain, senses
and a miraculous body
built for anything I want to do,
content, un-hurting.
I love it here.
This is where I live.
I don't want to leave.
I shall stay here until I die.

LATE AFTERNOON   *8/76*

The sun feels good on my skin.
It makes it glow.
It draws it out.
I soak up vitamin D.
When I turn on my side,
the sun warms me.
It sends loving rays to wash my body.
Laving rays, yellow and gold,
shimmering down,
playing on my back and thighs,
warming my buttocks

through my swimsuit.
The light from the sun
plays about the sand and towel, my hat.
It heats my glasses frames.
Effortlessly, my watch ticks.

I relax.

I doze.

The striving goes from my body.
My lids are heavy and I drift and dream.
My finite thoughts turn infinite.
I am logical in my thinking until
dimly aware I'm not logical at all,
I fall into sound sleep.
And the golden, laving, loving sun's rays
play on my back,
and the sun moves a noiseless notch to the west,
and I do not perceive that it does so,
for I am no longer present.
I am repairing my body.
My heart is lightly stroking,
sending warm blood to repair,
maintain, wash and clean,
and I am unaware and do not exist.

....

I stir with a breeze that cools my side.
I sleep on.
I awaken, cold.
The sun, farther in the west,
has slipped behind a cloud.
The golden rays no longer dance upon my skin.
In place of the rays,
a playing breeze

eddies in the hollows and contours of my body.
Goose bumps raise on my arms, back and thighs.
It is time to leave.
My skin is both burnt and cold.
I wipe the sand from my legs, stomach, chest
and pick up my towel.
I leave, feet in the cooling sand.

I WAIT   *8/76*

*M*y idle hands
are filled with blood.
My heart beats
lethargically.
I am lethargic.
I think,
not.
I am.
I know.
I see.
I feel my fat hand's
hot blood.
I wait.

I wait in a tiny seat
among thousands
my one wish
to be alone.
What myriad
series of circumstances,
agreements,

commitments,
habit patterns,
have produced this bored being?
This being
of discontent
with hot blood hands
among thousands
wishing for aloneness.

I wait.

HEAVEN *8/76*

I climbed the highest pinnacle
and leaping, rent the clouds
to peer at blue-black heaven
and a single, brittle star.

READY TO STRIKE *8/76*

I listen to traffic,
birds,
heavy sighs,
singing rails on railroad ties.

I test my eyes down the tracks
and see the convergence?

Where in the distance
do steel rails meet?

Do my eyes,
as yours,
come to a point?

Is the point of my mind
clear, alert, attentive, wise,

ready to strike,
should the occasion arise?

Would you believe it is?
No? Oh, well!

THE END *8/76*

Blue grass
red trees
spring breeze
clean glass
wrinkled knees
large fees
yellow bees
hot gas
golf tees
and galaxies
will soon pass.

WHAT THE HELL AM I DOING HERE?   *12/76*

What the hell am I doing here?
I take off my shoes
and fall apart.
I drink coffee for lunch,
spill off at the mouth.
Wired for sound,
I start to fly.
Sing all day long
eloquent tunes
of my own genius.
I play the role.
Am daring.
Am dashing.
Am devil-may-care.
'Til I crash,
like now,
with my shoes off,
I fall apart
and ask myself,
What the hell am I doing here?

EXTRAS   *12/76*

Tendency

There is
an overwhelmingly

tendency
within the
human race
to ingest food.

Planting Seeds

*I*f I plant a seed
a plant will grow
and bear a fruit
which I must eat.

It is prudent
I do not plant
a bitter seed.

Caring

*T*he universe
is incapable
of worry,
and therefore,
cares not
what I do.

I, of course,
care.

What We Need

*W*e need
a Basso-*Buffuno*.

Meaning?

*I*n order to say what you mean
you have to know what you mean.

EDGE OF THE DEAD *12/77*

*T*o live in a world
of quivers and gurgles
of clackings of bones
and movings of juices
and nails dug deep in the dirt.
To live in a world
of monotonous heartbeats
alone in a blackness
of cycling passions
and effortful strivings
lost in the midst of the earth.
To inhabit a bed
at the edge of the dead
alive without knowing you live.
A cog in a scheme
in a nameless dream
unable to weep,
in a lethargy
not quite sleep.

HOT WIND *12/76*

Unconfined,
the hot, untimely wind
comes whispering and moaning,
comes crying through the grasses
and brittle chaparral.

Unheedfully she's blowing.
She bows her head
and pressures
toward the sea.

She'll antagonize
and tease it,
whip it into foam,
and then will feign
a hurricane
to drive her humor home.

Whimsically,
she'll change her course
and run about a mile
to mingle with
the gentler winds
that play about the isle,
and there to doze
in light repose
and rest a little while.

WRITING IS A PRIVATE THING *12/76*

For writing
is a private thing
and should be indulged
alone.

Where one can think,
and dream,
and tour one's mind.

Roaming the windblown fields
of daisies and grass,
visiting lands with ice-blue skies,
and on a train,
rocketing across the baron highlands
in strange, fog-bound country,
remembering a long-dead
childhood friend.
But here in the crowd
you can't let go.
Writing is really
a private thing.

CREATOR *12/76*

Laughing
the laugh
of the great

creator,
a dwarf
with a large
sense of humor
and
very large
feet,
created
a universe
for himself
to eat.

BLACKDOG 2/77

*I*n the clarified night.
In the myriad white
of infinite suns and moons.

On the spine of a sinuous mountain,
spiraling into the gloom.
A glistening blackdog's
cosmic eye
pierces the night
with a shaft of sight,
singling out a tomb.

EXTRAS

Yellow Sky

The yellow sky was long since dead
and purple dreams were in my head.

Stylistic Grace

She walks with stylistic grace,
others mirrored in her face.

Coffee Anyone?

From the pinnacles
of lucid thought
to cottony doldrums
of discontent,
I come off coffee.

What's a Mil?

What's a mil,
or even a bil?
You're over the hill.
Take a pill.

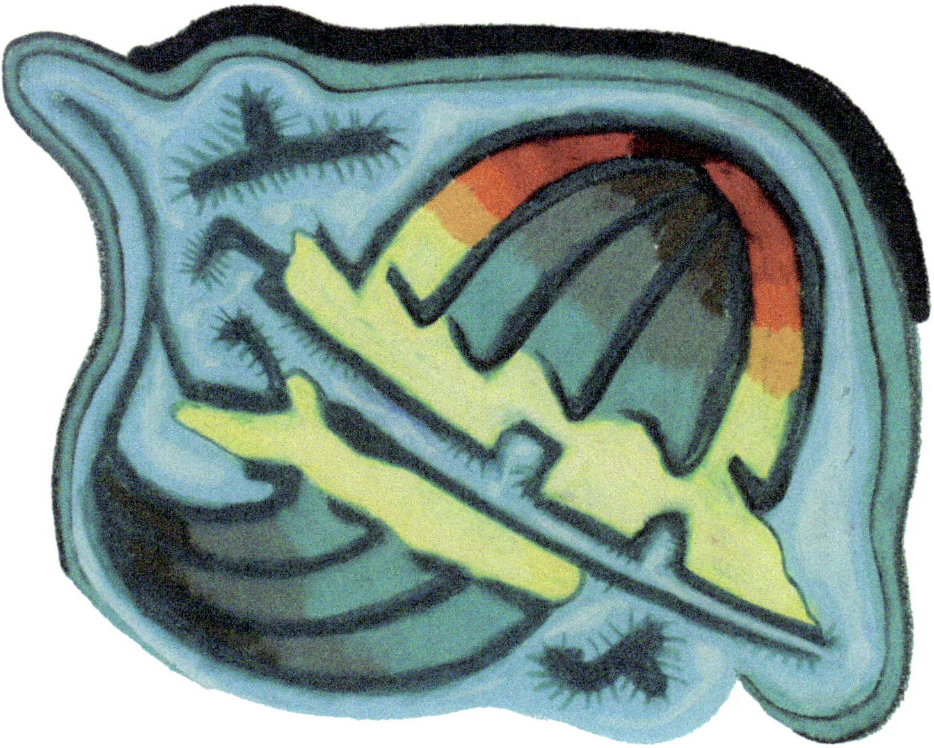

Eight

KORFU IMPRESSIONS　　　　　　　　　　　　　　　2/77

Soft petaled flowers
dance in fields,
cousins, brothers, sisters, friends,
they rule the land,
and smile through summer sun,
the early light,
the fog, the rain,
the flowing night.

Hoary, ancient, great.
Strong of trunk
firm of limb,
thick of leaf,

the Olive trees
bear abundant fruit,
and bestow wise consul
to the flowers in the field.

Seven fathoms deep,
the luminescent bay,
(a rich and royal hue)
team with fish,
staple of the peasant's dish.
A beach of polished stones,
some the shape and size of eggs,
brilliant in the sun,
but on a moonlit night,
mysteriously bright.

The fort, obscured by vines,
massive, sloping walls of stone,
rising from the silent sea,
indistinguishable from land,
a culmination of the earth.

Seventeen leagues from the sea,
and two or three above,
a toothless hag smiles at me,
her grinning husband, too.
She reaches out a bony hand,
uttering guttural noises
from her native land.

They guard the dead-stone village
with its dead-stone church
and petrified bell.
The grass, waste high,
where once were streets.
The town alive with ghosts.
The hag and husband,
wrinkled hosts.

Soft the petaled flowers
proliferate the land,
proof that Korfu likes itself,
as if it all were planned.

MORE NOTHING 2/77

I shall proclaim it to the hills,
sing it to the flowers in the fields,
shout it to the multitudes
that gather in the streets.
It shall be heard,
my nothing.

For I <u>will</u> have it heard.
I shall cry it to the gull
that hovers on the wind,
and to the stalwart trees.
(I'll bring them to their knees.)
I'll bring my message softly,
to the violets in bloom
that arch their dainty heads
to escape the forest gloom.
I'll whisper it to frogs and snails.
(Tie a message to their tails.)
They'll know the tale that I must tell,
my nothing.

And when the winter winds
come whistling through the fields,
come crying through the backyards

and open country fields,
and then the sloping snowdrifts
and crisp and crystal night
comes settling on the surface
on some special starlit night,
I'll stand alone and think,
project my message strong and clear
so all the universe will hear it,
(to me it's very dear)
my nothing.

PLEASE DO IT! *2/77*

HELP! HELP ME! I've been calling for days.
Won't someone please come to my aid?
I'm bleeding to death by the phone!

> *I'm here. Don't be afraid.*
> *I came as soon as I heard your cries.*
> *What's wrong?*

I'm in horrible pain and bleeding to death by the phone!
> *Can you talk?*

Yes.
> *Can you move your arms?*

Yes.
> *Can you hear?*

Yes.
> *Can you think? Can you read?*
> *Can you see? Can you feel?*

Yes. Yes. Yes. Yes.

But you're in pain and bleeding to death by the phone?
Yes.
Why didn't you call the Doctor?

I was waiting for you to do it.

ONE TASK FINISHED (An Epic)   *2/77*

I have finished what I set out to do.
It has been seven months since I started my task.
Occasionally my work went swiftly
as it does when I play or do what I like.
At other times the minutes seemed like hours
and the hours seemed like days.
The paragraphs I have spoken.
The paragraphs I have written,

    I cannot count or remember.
The gestures I have used
and facial expressions used
to get across an idea, meaning, or feeling,
    I cannot count or remember.
The breakfasts, lunches, dinners I have consumed,
the clinking of eating utensils,
the clean clothes I have soiled and washed,
    cannot be counted or remembered.
And tales I have told to my wife and children,
and attitudes, either happy or sad,
    or tired or hostile, or humorous,
and the attitudes I have evoked in my family, or provoked
    cannot be counted or remembered.

The examples I have set, either good or bad,
the energy that has passed through me and was used by me
from sleep to food to action to excrement,
the animals and plants I have caused to die
by my need for them,
the foliage, fungus, bacteria,
that now live solely because of me
    cannot be counted or remembered.
The dawns, the arching of the daily sun,
the sunsets that have set, the moon chasing Venus
or Venus chasing moon and the myriad starlit positions
with respect to each other during the time
of my seven month task,
and the changes in the political atmosphere in this country,
and in all the countries of the world,
and the births of babies, and the deaths of the elderly,
and those fighting for their lives in hospitals,
or in countries that have insufficient food,
    cannot be counted or remembered.
And the murders and heroic acts in saving people
or animals, or on the sea or natural countryside,
the rainstorms, the draughts, the hurricanes, snowstorms,
blizzards, cyclones, fogs, sleet, white-outs, calms,
that have occurred, while I was completing my task
    are impossible to total.
The minute erosion of all mountain ranges and hills,
the minute increase in ocean salinity
resulting from salt in streams rambling into the sea,
my own irrevocable aging,
the minute deepening of lines in my face,
and the deepening of lines in the faces of others,
the minute maturing of my own and others personalities,
    cannot be counted or remembered.
All these things and infinitely more,
took place while I was completing my task.
And though at times, it was difficult,
    I'm glad I completed it.

I WISH TO DO IT MY WAY

*B*ut I must do it my way.

>*Can you not see the value in my way?*

I can.

>*I had another type of life for you.*

I'm sorry.

>*You are part of my dreams and expectations.*

I sense that.

>*I need you to be the way I had expected.*

I cannot.

>*My plan is perfect for you.*

I must be true to myself.

>*You'll be happier doing it my way.*

What is your way?

>*Hocus, pocus, dominocus, twenty-three skidoo.*

That's senseless.

>*Not from my standpoint.*

It is from mine.

Please, do it my way. For God's sake! What's the big deal?

I'd give up my life.

It would be another kind of life, that's all.

If you persist, I will become angry.

Don't you want my love?

Not at the price.

I'll never see you again.

Goodbye.

Ok! What's your way?

Furry things. Tree life. Silly in the breeze.

Is it fun?

I like it.

Maybe I'll try it.

WAITING FOR A DAUGHTER   2/77

Twinkling tones of tear-shaped glasses
brighten the eyes of the local lasses.

Eight 163

A steaming volcano of vegetable soup.
Simple salt and pepper twins
with silver heads and finger holes.

Someone sorting silverware
and napkin covered rolls.
An ice cold cracker in a crinkly wrapper.

"Basically, I believe..."

The rippling song's refrain,

"I wish you wouldn't leave..."

My effort all in vain.

Table tops in tile shimmer in the sun.
A kerosene lamp
with a petrified wick.
An empty bowl
and a sandwich stick.

A single yellow jonquil listens to my heart.

An elemental shape,
cool and smooth to touch.
Oh, my darling daughter,
I love you very much.

A CHILD'S PAINTING *3/77*

A sated orange sun
edged in black

appears in the night.
Hidden holes in rocks are lit.
Creeping things recede.
Creatures of night water
scurry to the deep.
Five black crows,
startled,
wing their separate ways.
One black cloud,
tinged in orange,
holds its stolen place.

PHOBOS AND DIEMOS   *3/77*

*P*hobos and Diemos
(bouldery moons)
skimming the surface of Mars.
Devil-dogs of the airless night.
Parasites of the warring God,
scarred, pitted, damned,
hurtle along through a hellish light.

THE ONE TO CALL HERSELF   *3/77*

I have a daughter
who would find herself

if she knew where to look.
She keeps her eyes open wide
and though she is everywhere,
glimpses only now and then
that familiar face,
that image pleasing,
that person she would recognize,
that one to call herself.

THE ANSWER 4/77

I have a book called The Answer,
but I never read it.
It lies on my desk in the corner.
It gathers dust.
The jacket curls.
I long to know what's in it,
but I have never once reached for it.

At night, sometimes I cannot sleep.
My head spins.
I try to think things out.
I am thoroughly at loss.
*(Straws on the wind,
leaves on the tide.)*

My answer book lies, inert,
on the corner of my desk,
lent by a well meaning friend.
Its cover bears the title,
The Answer.

It will explain everything, fine,
that I need to know.
And I desperately need to know.

When I complain,
as I usually do,
my friend says,
"Please open the book."
<u>The Answer.</u>

I always plan to.
I *"plan"* to right now.

When the mood strikes me right.
When the stars are aligned in a beautiful design.
When the moon whispers to me during an eclipse.
When night winds promise rain on the 5th of December.
I do have the answer in my personal possession.
It's in that book, there by the door,
<u>The Answer,</u>
all of it written,
what I'm going to know.

I have never reached for it.
At times I do not think I see it.

Perhaps I don't want
my friend's answer.
His may be dull.

What if mine were
a rampageous river,
begging to be followed,
up the frigid canyons,
in the hollows of the turns,
through the mountains
and the meadows,
bright with flowers.

The answer book's a thief,
robs me of discovery.

I must learn <u>not</u> to ask
for what I <u>don't</u> want to know.

DREAM, DISCOVERY, INSIGHT 4/77

*M*y newly tanned face
came off in my dream.
I reached at the hairline and pulled at the skin.
The skin and my face peeled slowly away.
First one side,
carefully, slowly,
I peeled it back.
Beneath was a new, clean, younger skin,
a new person, me, with shining eyes.
I pulled at the top of my scalp.
I peeled the skin off my face,
slowly, deliberately, until it all came off
like a long, limp mask with hair attached.

As I held it to show a horrified friend,
it became repulsive, rotten,
a ghastly, detached mask
with holes for eyes, mouth, and nose.

I looked at my face in the mirror.
It was black, diseased.
I was afraid!

I reached to pull the black skin off.
My chin crumpled like black cottage cheese
and threatened to fall to the floor.

I peeled again at my hideous mask
and pulled it once more away.
In the mirror, this time,
a new face with healthy, pink skin,
eyes black and shining
and hair glistening,
greeted my eyes.
Astounded, I gazed at my own new face,
different from the old.
My own new self.

I DRIFT IN A WAKING DREAM 9/77

I drift in a waking dream.
I walk with my heart.
I glide in cool shadows
of roses and ferns.
I leap to clouds
and descend,
a fluttering rain,
born on the down
of a delicate air
with fragrance
as rich as my love.
A welcome storm.
I sweep the grass
of a quiet valley
and merge in delight

with tall, green shoots.
I trickle and run,
swirl and tumble.
I play with clarity,
light,
and jewel like stones.
I run to the sea
and merging,
drift in a waking dream.

UNDECIDED *12/77*

*T*he river, slowing,
comes to an uncertain stop,
threatens to tip and flow backward.

The air is stiff.
A branch doesn't move.
A bubble doesn't burst.

A baby's breath of wind
tickles the sky and clouds
painted on the surface,
but has no affect.

The sun smiles grease.
The trees hang limp.
A fisherman sucks his breath.

The weight of the river is balanced,
nervous, threatening,
undecided.

CHANGE   *12/77*

Change has me from the inside.
It's been coming long
like growth of moss
on cypress trees
or coral rocks
in southern seas.
I'm filled with change
like a beaker of steam.

It flows behind my eyes and mouth.
It penetrates my bones and skin.
It infiltrates each nerve and vein.
It rules me from within.

I cough mist
and wisps curl from my nose
like silent spiral ghosts.

But change to what?

I DO GET UP   *12/77*

The dawning sun
comes full upon my face,
and with its heat,
a rush of blood
infuses every vein.

Jumbled dreams
come rapidly to a close,
and while I doze
the wind comes fresh,
flying free,
it hums through the Sumac
and bottle-brush tree.

Nadia's Theme
From Amanda's room,
and tapping on the floor
and children's morning voices
penetrate the door.

My love sleeps on
and though I'm charged
and ready to act,
I'm confused on the fact
of the eternal order
of changing things,
growth of our children,
my irrevocable aging.
The invincible life
on our planet raging.

The challenge of yet another day
in the stream of countless days.

With blood I'm fused,
and yet, confused.

Futility feelings
occur in my dealings.

The insistent sun,
the patient wind,
the perfect good,
the perfect bad.

The all there is!

I do get up.

ELECTRIFIED   *12/77*

On a drifting mountainside,
the air, ominous, thick,
we suck our breath.

Approaching thunder grumbles.
Birds, bees, hide in holes.
Insects freeze.
In silence,
the clouds billow up.

The atmosphere is yellow,
dried,
golden as an aura,
electrified.

Our body's hair stands on end.
The Monday morning paper said,

*"Four struck dead!
Burns on feet and head!"*

Our tongues, white,
we leave in dread.

EXTRAS *12/77*

Strained Silence

The Iris haughtily stormed away,
she went for a walk by the sea.

The Rose was piqued
and her strong perfume
compelled a bumblebee.

The Dandelion sillily
waved her hands
and tried to smile it away,

but the air was dense
and the flowers were tense,
and I didn't know what to say.

The Clock

I'd like to sock
The ever-present clock.

Which Category are You?

Category I

Miss Universe.
Independently wealthy,
tubes tied,
don't give a shit!

or Category II

Miss close-up view of a bat's head.
Stone broke.
Ten kids.
Try like a son-of-a-bitch.

How to be simple.

*V*olume 12-B

Poetry Reading by Ima Klutz

*T*he birdies, blue,
fly all day long
up *in* the sunny sky.

The froggies, green,
gaze up at them
and wish that *they* could fly.

The doggies, brown,
frisk around
and *with* a little sigh,
reach deep into their pockets
for a piece of pecan pie.

The kitties, white,
Were just a sight,
And looked a *little* pa.....*BANG! BANG! BANG!*

Head Down

I race, head down,
across a broken town.

Heart

I stand
with a solid-tree heart.

Roots and Shoots

*F*rom old roots,
tender shoots.

SEEDS OF MYSELF 12/77

*S*oft my wind
that loves the fields
comes airily through my face.
I'll forget my race with ghosts of beings
wishing they were me.
I must be free
to live in a land
of color and line
as rich as my dream,
to ride on a musical beam
as bright as the joy in my heart,
and listen to rhymes
of dandelions
in the warmth of a mid-spring day,
to play in between
Venus and Moon
and ride on the back
of a fearful night.

(It is my right.)
To love the face
and thoughtful grace
of a woman who's much like me,
so the tree of my being
shall bear sweet fruit
and the seeds of myself
take root.

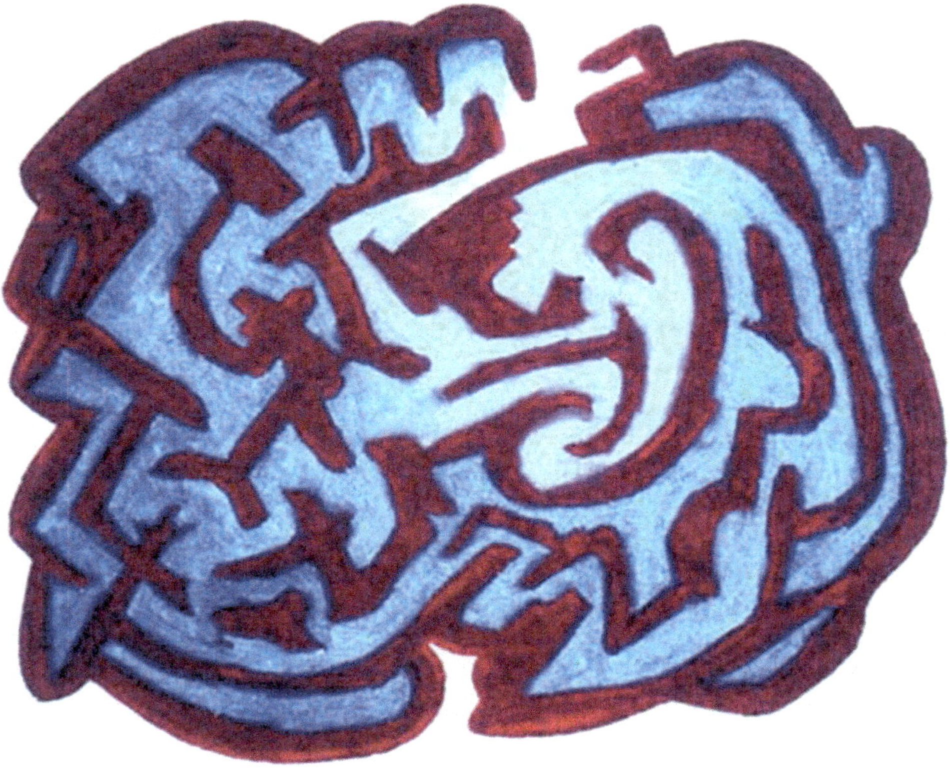

Nine

MING AND MANG 12/77

*M*ang is huge with fire for eyes,
with stones for feet,
and hooks for hands.
He walks on tree-stump legs,
and slices clouds
with a black-night sword.
Ming, with armored jaw
and iron-spiked toes,
presses them deep
in the river's mud.
His passions in cycles,
weak as a willow,

strong as a storm,
awaits the attack.
Mang advances, sword held high.
Ming awaits, afraid to die.
The clatter of battle
shatters all peace.
The sun hangs limp.
The moon is red.
The flowers in the fields are dead.
And the blood of Mang,
and the blood of Ming,
mingle in a thick-snake stream,
that writhing, burns to the sea
where the surge and pull
of deep-cut currents
scatter it, red, to every shore
for all the world to see.
The living nations hands,
with black-knit gloves,
clasp their bloodied eyes
and place their leaden skulls
between their useless thighs.
And then, when eternities have passed,
on some witless, arbitrary day,
the sun, returning full and round,
casts a healing ray,
separates the two,
declares a fighting stay.
Mang, half dead, lies in blood.
Ming, half alive, crawls away.
Vivid in parting,
the memories of pain
do not last,
but are all in vain.

CORRECT AND TRUE   *12/77*

Correct and true,
permanent unshakable
love,
sweet solid love,
flows through your sweet body,
generating a binding energy,
that, flowing, returns
and binds my own.

MY HEART SANG YOUR SONG   *12/77*

I missed you today,
but my heart sang your song.
It said,
you are my pal,
my buddy,
my counterpart found,
my final friend.
To think we have existed
on parallel courses
through all these years.
If only I'd known.
I feel chosen as the special one,
selected for another chance,
released unexpected,
and allowed to return,
as from a distant war.

My soul mate,
my mirror image,
my very own beauty,
to hold,
to love.
It is with you
I wish to share
the vitality of my years,
for I only live when you are near.
I long for you.
I am lonely for you.
I want you.
I must fill my empty space with you,
for when you are gone,
I'm not whole.
My own.
My true love.
My life.
To be with you
is to have a growing love.
My heart was wound tight
with many strings
for many years.
You have released me
with but a single tug.
I love your eyes,
your lids,
your lashes.
I love your fingertips and toes
and the nape of your neck.
They are made for me to kiss.
I want you.
I long for you.
I love you.

DESPERATE

I am desperate
to tell my stories.
To share a me,
I, only, know.
I am desperate to live
by telling
the moments of my great events,
however small.
I am desperate to see
seeds of my unique tree
grow startling to maturity.
I am desperate,
too, to listen
to stories no one else can hear.
To see the richness
of another's *"great events."*
The ones that pass in grayish light,
but in the telling,
told with passion,
come to life
in red and green and white.
I m desperate to tell,
and after telling,
desperate to be told.

DESTRUCTIVE HABITS 2/78

Destructive habits never stop,
but keep on growing.
Like a stubborn weed
that ever firmly roots,
ever stronger are its shoots.
When it's cut
low on the stem,
the roots still send the sap,
begin to mend,
and soon that stubborn habit-weed
is growing once again.
To get at the root takes digging.
The root of the habit must die.
Don't sever the stem.
Work at the root.
The root of the habit must die.

WORDS WILL SAVE ME 2/78

Words will save me.
Words of wisdom,
life and death and love.
Words of green grass growing,
or brown wet leaves
on damp black earth.
Words like stars,
that one by one

in needlepoint appear
when twilight turns to night.
Words that undulate,
    and dip,
    and rise,
along the silent surface
of a gently flowing sea.
Words to change the course of living.
Words on which to build a dream.
Words of irony and fate.
Words that make you cry.
Words of unmitigated hate.
Words that make you try.
    I'll try.
    For time is life
    and life is time,
    and time is me
    and time is you.
Words will let me live my life.
Words will get me through.

ON BEING FREE   2/78

I run through forests
racing trunks
on needles
soft as down.

I leap branches,
jump streams,
hurtle stones.

I run with perfect ease
and grace,
in perfect time,
and perfect rhythm,
for I am a man with
a perfect purpose.

I am clouds and sky,
wild yellow roses
in tall green grass,
a lover of food and sleep,
women and song.

I run like the wind
combing the field
on some black night
and never am tired.

I am infinite variety,
leaves on the tree,
feathers on the wing,
scales in the murk
of some lost sea.

I never stop inhaling.
My lungs are big as buildings.
I only breathe out when I want,
and that for purest pleasure.

I am big and free,
long of arm,
long of torso,
hip and thigh.

I swim oceans,
climb mountains.
I fly through the air,
and sing with birds.

Nine

I love it here.
It's made for me,
my world.
It has infinite variety.

I rise and float.
I sing a two day song.
I play for as long as a year,
if I want,
and never get tired.

I am a meteoric boulder,
pea sized,
tumbling in a shallow stream.

I lie in wait for a year,
or doze and dream,
perfectly content.

Darkness doesn't bother me,
nor does the desert air.

Mighty rainstorms are my home.
I wish they'd never end,
for I have time.

I do not age,
but seemingly grow younger
with every passing day.

The pathway clears itself before me.
Giant pines move their trunks
to avoid my stride.

Mountains open as I approach,
and when I'm gone,
close themselves behind.

I wade the seas,
and visit islands.
The sea turtle is my friend.
We swim together,
arm and fin,
in silent harmony.

I follow the whale
to hidden depths,
and linger just a while.

I sift my fingers
through silts of ages
in the pitch of the Japanese trench.

I calibrate the shifts
of continental plates
before I go to lunch.

I marvel at a grain of sand
glistening in the sun.

Or a quiet tear.
Or a drop of dew.
Or a raindrop,
cool and clear.

I love my private world,
and my perfect purpose.
The purpose of being.

WITH APOLOGIES TO T. S. ELIOT 2/78

"But though I have wept and fasted, wept and prayed,
Though I have seen my head *(grown slightly bald)*
brought in upon a platter,
I am no prophet-and here's no great matter.

I have seen the moment of my greatness flicker,
and I have seen the Eternal Footman
hold my coat, and snicker,
and in short, ..."
        Check which...

        ____ *I was afraid.*

        ____ *I was not afraid.*

HANGING IN 2/78

My love for you,
on the westerly wind,
hangs in like a kite.
.

The thought of you
separates each action
of my day.

My heart is strong.
My blood is rich,

and longs to mingle
with your own.

You taunt me,
dare me,
then comply.

I love to be kissed
by a smiling eye.

You insinuate
yourself in me.

The one of you
and the one of me
is the one
of us.

FINITE SCHEME   *2/78*

I love those other
searching lips.
The ones through which
are made the absolute union,
the solid joining,
one to one,
of loving mates.
The ones through which
the multi-layered
songs of ages
rejoice on earth.

The ones for which
so perfectly
a man is made
within this finite scheme.

I SEE YOU TRY TO HEAL MY HEART 2/78

I see you try to heal my heart,
my heart now laid so bare.
My wound, however,
will not close,
but gapes upon the air.

I have a friend
with soothing hands
that, cool with love,
holds me firm,
my wounded heart.

Rush away,
kiss away,
fly away, my pain.

I hope to have my hateful heart
loving once again.

CAN YOU LET ME GO?

Can you let me go into the land of my own love?
Land I have never seen except in dreams?
Land I have longed for through these long years,
as I long for my fingers and eyes?
The soft, brown, precious eyes of a gentle dog?
Can you let me go to my love,
as the eye of the dog is loved, is precious to him?
Can you keep me from my eye, my love,
when I long to see, as I long for my hands?
Can you let me find my life's longing
in this, my later life and the backs of my wrinkled hands?
Can you let me be in that state you claim you've had
for lo these years?
May I find my only love, while yet there's time,
to live in the land of my loving self?
To sing the song I have longed to sing,
for just this once, in these final years?
To find my longing, to find my life.
To find that love, heavy upon me?
That love so long overdue, over ripe, so long,
so longing for use?
Can you find in your own true heart
the strength, the love to open the gate?
To let me run in the grass, hills,
trees, love of a later life?
I'd love you so.

OH, ANGUISH!

Oh, anguish
    on letting you go.
Your own sweet body,
    so used to mine.
Your breasts and hips,
those loving thighs,
those feet I've held in mine,
    the full, ripe flow
    of your loving form
    I know like my soul.
How can I let you go?
Discard that smile,
    those eyes that loved me,
    (love me?)
through laughter and spice
    of an eager, early life,
through anguished nights
    of our children's years,
    (and fears)
through buildings
    and songs,
through fire and rainstorms,
    and myriad ways
    of our sunlit days.
We lived as a key in a lock
    our allotted time.
How can I let those wistful eyes
    fade into mist and time?
I love you
    as my feet firmly planted,
    as I breathe,
    as I see,
as I feel my heart,

heavy at the thought
of letting you go.
Oh, anguish!

I CARE   *4/78*

I care.
I do care.
I really do care.
I care! I care!

So what?

I'll hurt them,
    and then they'll grow.
And I'll hurt myself,
    and then *I'll* grow.
But can we all break through
this strange,
divided,
dark period
(with promise of heartache)
(with promise of fulfillment)
into a calm,
steady,
peaceful,
land of our own contentment?
Are we *all* really working toward this
    in our subconscious way?

The road
    has many turns,
    many surprises,
    many thrill's,
    many disguises.

NO!   *4/78*

A day or two ago,
about to make love,
I asked,
*"Would you please leave your necklace on,
the one I gave you, nothing else?"*
So lovely,
so enticing,
so rich and desirable,
so loving.
You said, *"No."*
without a thought,
and took it off,
afraid you'd break it.

GROWTH   *4/78*

I am tired.
I am sleepy.

I am exhausted.
My situation
ties on me a heavy weight,
a sorrow,
and I cannot be free,
though it is the state I long for.
The way to freedom is pain,
and I'm in the midst.
How did I come to these dark woods?
By living my life.
By opening my eyes.
Who can tell
when they'll wake from a dream,
or how they'll cope
with a new real life?
I wait, with solemn face,
to see what I will do.
(I don't know.)
I hope not to feel badly
when I think of myself,
whenever it's done,
whatever I do.
And I hope that my friends,
with sympathy and love,
will all gather around
my warped root.
Forgive me,
I cannot grow otherwise.

PARALLAX POWER

*B*ut, if you know
what I know,
then that would be
the most definite,
the most possible,
the most coherent
and real
dream-like occurrence
in the history
of our age.
To know
as I know,
To feel as I feel
the deep,
exuding,
unrelenting,
"Parallax"
to the 14th power.
To indulge
in the depths
of feeling
and being.
To talk
to birds
and dogs
and worms.
To say
just that utmost
that comes
to all people.
Don't be alarmed.
This could never happen to you,
unless you were to see

as I see.
Then the powers
would strike out
and you, too,
would be engulfed,
as so many
of our unfortunate souls
in the past
have met their deliverance.
So,
seek ye the finite,
the real,
the truly heroic lands
or your lost truth,

"Algernon!"

and be like me.
Then tell the world.
Yeh! Preach to all nations,
all people,
all beings.
Tell them of your feelings
in this time
of our discontent.
Be with them
and say,
as you would want
to say to me,
that <u>occurrence</u>
is the best example.
And treat it not
with sympathy,
but rather
as it should be treated.
That is to say,
with extreme empathy

and un-towardness.
I have found it,
and so will you.
The everlasting,
soul-searching,
deep breathing,
mentally strong,
heartfelt beating,
wanderlust,
that lies hidden
and unknown
within every breast.
I say, *"Look for it!"*
Ferret it out!
And when it is clear,
and when you have finished,
find it!
Then,
as I stand here,
brazen in my wisdom,
you will have it, too,
as I do.

Look now!

IN DEADLY EARNEST *4/78*

*I*n deadly earnest
I play with lives.
I dangle them on my string.
Solemnly,

I watch them take me in,
their loving eyes,
their wistful eyes,
their laughing eyes,
their crying eyes,
and I,
with serious countenance,
telling myself I long for truth,
blunder my way,
push my white tendril up
through crumbly earth
disturbing rocks,
sand, and shiny pebbles,
awkward,
ugly,
wandering,
wondering
how I shall get through to real growth.
When shall I get a new green leaf,
my first?
This rooting takes so long.
I must live through this period
with patience,
frustration,
longing,
fear for myself,
fear for others.
I must get through this rooting
before I can grow with ease.

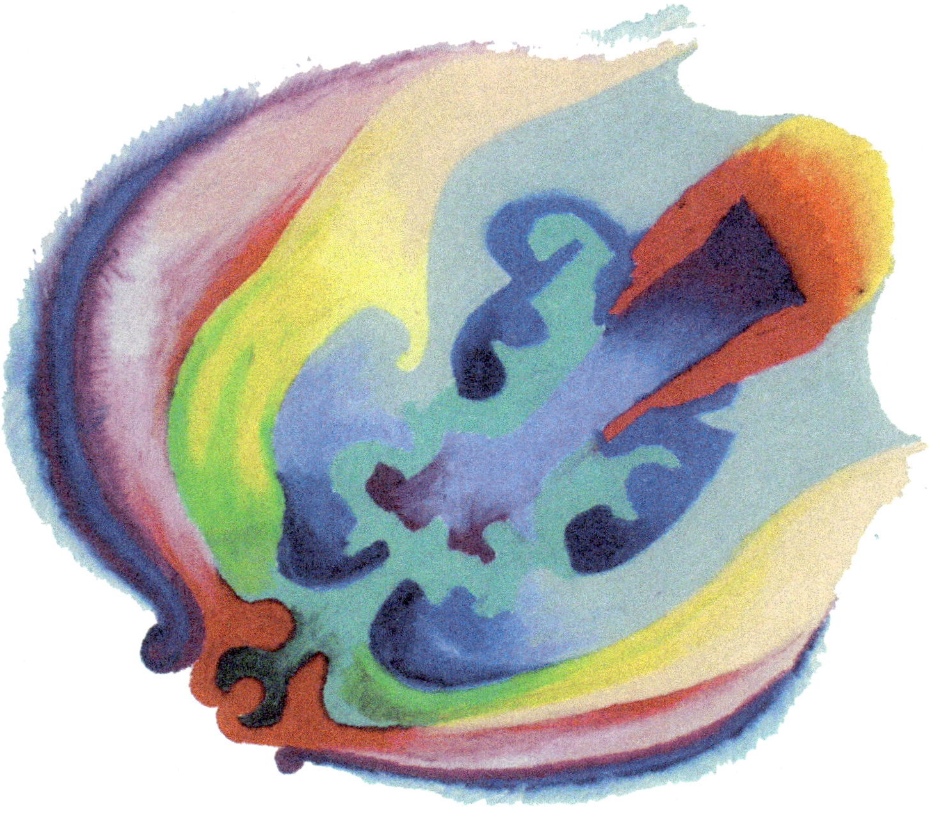

Ten

EXTRAS 4/78

Shiver Me Timbers

"Shiver me timbers!"
she said,
so I did just that!

Wow, Dad!

Daughter *(looking at old photo)*
"Wow, Dad, you were once great looking. What happened?"
Dad   "Face went bad."

To Whom it May Concern:

I hereby authorize you
to take over in those areas
wherein I've failed.

Brains of Paper

*B*rains made of paper.
I wadded them up, *(the papers)*
and shoved them through my ears.
Viveka says, *"Got a match?"*

Finding Oneself

I could find myself
if I only knew where to look.

Trigger of Love

I've got my finger
on the trigger of love.

NOW, IN DARK SHADOWS PLAYNG   *5/78*

*N*ow,
in dark shadows playing,
light and shivering,

the infinite wind,
crossing limitless space,
infiltrates, fills,
lifts and settles,
'til brittle night
closes, turns the key,
and sadness descending
all the while,
graceful, gliding,
lifting, settling,
comes irrevocably
to stillness,
allows motionless-ness
to become the leaves,
the dark shadows,
light and quivering.

GREENNESS AND DEATH *5/78*

I live in greenness,
flashing-eye light
(purple against black)
night sky whose stars,
brisk, needle-pointed, icy,
stab the cold-steel-air,
swelling, filling, engulfing
the red-eye,
blue-nose,
white-ears ,
and head in tightness,
limiting fulfillment,

yet embracing,
(warm arms encircling)
head inclined,
and love in living,
and in death.

MORE OF THE SAME   5/78

Green and black,
tough, gnarled bark trunks
waited in space,
and roulette wheel moonlights
dazzled beings, who,
dizzy with birthing,
loving and dying,
passed through irrevocable time,
until, at last,
that false hope,
still breath,
pinpoint certification
arrived with pomp,
heralding repetition.
Beginnings and endings
merged,
and momentary eyes and heads
recognized that
a finite state is illusion,
and that
true God everlasting
is more of the same.

FLOWING AND SINKING   *5/78*

Flows and sinks,
rises,
then flowing again
and sinking.
Undulating.
As gray fish,
white stripe,
black, yellow,
pancake eye,
stares and leans
on thick, still, water,
element of tube-like rushes,
submerged,
slim as trees,
vertical, and fish,
motionless,
green and growing,
making vertical space,
cool and clear.
Perpendicular the rushes
and motionless,
between,
turns with a jerk,
red eye, black fin,
silver stripe.
A curious look.
A lightning jerk.
A darting.
Stillness and floating,
curiosity, inward.
Feeling cool
with juices flowing,
gasses bubbling.

POUNDING

*L*ead-heavy hands
pounding with purpose,
with rage, with anguish.
A blood crammed heart,
a ram-rod spirit,
and a soul with a promise.
It shatters the still,
thick-shadowed, cool earth,
with a promise.
A pounding in concert
with fist and heart
in rhythm and blood,
and beats to the stomach-rage
fouled with green.
A wounded soul
that pounds with purpose,
and knowing, and working it out,
and going along, and letting it out.
A continuous process.
A running the course.
A thunder cloud sounding.
A tree trunk pounding.
A finishing out.
A dying away.
A missed beat falling.
A heart beat stalling.
An ice blue knot
melting to red.
A lagging of pounding.
A falling, a sobbing.
A stopping.
A sobbing.

EMERGING *5/78*

*E*merging from the grass,
dark, it moved,
uncertain, the grass,
tall, green, unsteady,
then shifting,
a pawn of the wind.
It moved in the dark,
as stars,
piercing the back of the night
punctured the violet drop.
The green grass glowing,
illuminated from within,
spent it's iridescent force,
wavering, then blowing,
steady, then bending,
flowing, then stopping
in the cool night wind.
And emerging therefrom,
furry and black
with soft yellow eyes,
and curved black claws,
vicious, yet gentle,
but fearful,
the creature came forth,
and moving and twitching the grass,
made it's meticulous way
into the violent night.

OVER AND UNDER

When will the...
in the time of the oval shaped moon,
edge dipped in blood and swollen,
let out the stars,
in their infinite right,
to spread, engulfing,
proclaiming, encompassing?
And when they have found
and permeated
and infiltrated
and claimed,
then the right is theirs,
and theirs, alone,
and they remain solid,
immovable,
and glow with certainty
unequalled by men.
They are.
They claim.
They do.
For the stars are of the earth,
and none can dig under,
for they are under
as well as over,
and it would do us well
to ponder this thing
and take heed
and absorb this absolute fact
into our beings,
so that none can dig under us,
for we, also, are under
and over if once we see stars
as they truly are.

WHISTLING *5/78*

Whistling, he goes,
for he is sun
and barefoot on the earth
and rolled jeans
and tanned body
and he walks
and is under the wind
as well as the rain,
and is soaked,
but never is wet,
for he claims his space.
He knows as the wind
that the tree
in it's solid-state root
can reach to the pits of the earth
and strike to the sky as well
and fill every void,
and claim.
For it is.
And he is.
And both are,
and will be
and have been
and so shall we
if we do.

WAITING *5/78*

*1*300 + 2,762
equals minus 10
to the square root of tree,
which claims its space,
and rooting and sinking,
every tendril seeking,
every leaf a-quaking
on a 12 knot wind.
11 + 13 = 42,
or don't you think?
For I have eyes
and I can see,
and if I'm blind,
you'll marry me.
One and one is six.
Lonely I live,
waiting for thee.

QUIETLY, I WAIT *5/78*

I touch
as I touch not.
I reach
and reaching, reach.
I know what I know,
and then I do not.

For I am a king,
and oranges hang high,
heavy and ripe,
from an old orange tree.
Yet if I marry,
become one with the wind,
my love will be now,
and I'll die when I do.
    17 – 16 – 15 – 4
    Quietly, I wait,
    then open the door.

I REACH AND REACHING, REACH   *5/78*

I am next to,
but not quite.
I search inside.
I sink to depths,
and look within.

Round, red balls
of soft red fire
cling to the edge
of a black burnt tree
with leaves as green
and thick as green,
or greener.

This, I find
and nothing more.

I must descend
to a greater depth.

I must reach and reach,
and reaching,
reach.

GREEN STICK TREE 5/78

Deeply, I deep.
Here in the land
of one lost leaf
and amber sky,
lost in infinity's desert,
tired, looking for...
With hope,
I merge with the ...
and tingle and sleep,
and the great white dove,
wings outspread,
hangs in the sky
and will not speak,
but with loving eye.
I have entered here,
brought to this place,
and I like myself
and this in-between,
for over the mountain
is the land of my dream.
I walk with hope
and the iron-black crows

with hard, yellow eyes
and insulting calls,
unsettle me, now,
though I shall prevail
and move beyond
the green-stick tree
with buds all around.

THE ONLY *5/78*

This is the ...
with lightning rays
of soft, white light.
And in all the stop,
where shall we go?

When soft rain falls
and dew,
to dew-drop places go.
And rain,
and tree-trunks lie,
steeped in age,
heart-wood soft,
decayed.

Then will the ...
and I shall too.
For this is the ...
and the only ...
and it is made for me
and the dying trunk
and the green-stick tree.

IF I TRY

When will the ...
in the land of the ...
in that great,
ever-so infinity,
become a ...
and feel,
and know?
Stone sits quietly,
asleep, awake,
knowing,
not knowing,
hot, cold, in-between,
old, young,
rarely seen.
And when will ...
and how will it feel?
And should I?
For I am the ...
and I want to.
And if I try,
I will.

I CLAIM IT MINE

6/78

I have a ...
and the solid,
too, too heart
of the wood-nut tree,
spread, as if to the wind,
and growing,
claimed it's space,
as a giant hand
clasps the clouds
and wrings them dry
with the certainty of giants
striding in the wood.
Then, as if to ...
and the heaving
and swelling night,
and the coming and going
of the multi-colored stars,
the wind shifting
and sweeping,
slowing, then swooping,
the bird on the wind,
wings outstretching
and black, steady,
yet arching in strength,
moving, as lead,
broadly across the paper,
speeds through the heavens
and marks it mine.

MUSIC TALK *6/78*

The sounds reach me.
They have been traveling
from the opposite face of the earth,
and I hear them,
for my eardrums are sensitive
and pick the vibrations
from the stillness of the night.
They tell me that ...
and I answer them
and they reply
and I listen carefully
and we communicate,
for we are one with the other
and love conversation.
Sometimes we sing to each other
and the music,
to and fro,
crowds the airways.
Sometimes we weep
for the beauty of the sound,
for our listening is ...
and must be done,
if we are to know.

RARE GIFT

*F*or in the beginning
it was this way,
    when,
upon bending closely to the ground
and listening to tall grass,
    earth,
    dead leaves
    and worms,
the heart, the center,
throbbing powerfully,
let me know that ...
and I believed it
and raised my eyes to the blue heavens
and saw the clouds parting
and one lone star,
brighter than Venus,
shone upon me
and said to me,
    "You have been.
    You are.
    You shall become,
    before you die."
I kissed the earth
and wept
for this gift of love,
for never before have I ...
but always have I wanted ...
So rare is it, that ...
I need.
I want.
I love.

WINNIE

Winnie is a dog.
Do you love Winnie?
Yes.
Does Winnie love you?
Yes.
Is Winnie a lucky dog?
Yes.
Winnie, big, black,
clear yellow eyes
that burn into your own.
Intelligent, sensitive.
Strength to range a thousand miles.
Lies under the bed
all day long.
A pat in the morning,
good dog, nice dog.
A pat in the evening,
nice dog, good dog.
And the hours slip by,
minute by minute,
thick as incense
through the long afternoon.
A pat in the evening.
Good dog.
A pat in the morning.
Nice dog.
Winnie broke loose.
Through tall sage
and grease-wood
she bounded,
hot on the trail.
Tail up, nose down,
she followed the ground.

Then half-mile away to the Center
to play by the swings,
scuff sand with children.
Then half-mile away to the creek
she sloshed through bulrushes,
algae and mud.
She lapped the clear water
and went for a swim,
her powerful muscles
glistening in the sun.
A good shake, head, body, tail,
then through a field of flowers
and on to the road,
where someone found her,
lost, and phoned her in.
Guilt-ridden Winnie,
picked up in the car.
Shame!
Into the house
with the dog-door shut.
And the heavy afternoon
under the bed.
The dozing,
the stretching,
the yawning,
the yearning.
A pat in the evening.
Good dog, nice dog.
And slow clocks tick.
And restless dreams.
And laboring through the night.
Oh, lucky, lucky Winnie.
oh, lucky dog.
For whom is the dog?

CLOSED

Sometimes I ...
then I ...
and don't want to
and I shut up tight
and wrap strings about myself,
and never come out,
    unless I am,
with infinite care,
for a long, long time,
    coaxed,
and then with reluctance.
But then if ...
and I don't want to,
I wrap myself again,
this time for keeps.
So watch out for me.
For I am ...
Though I probably shouldn't be.
But don't.
Unless you want ...
Closed.

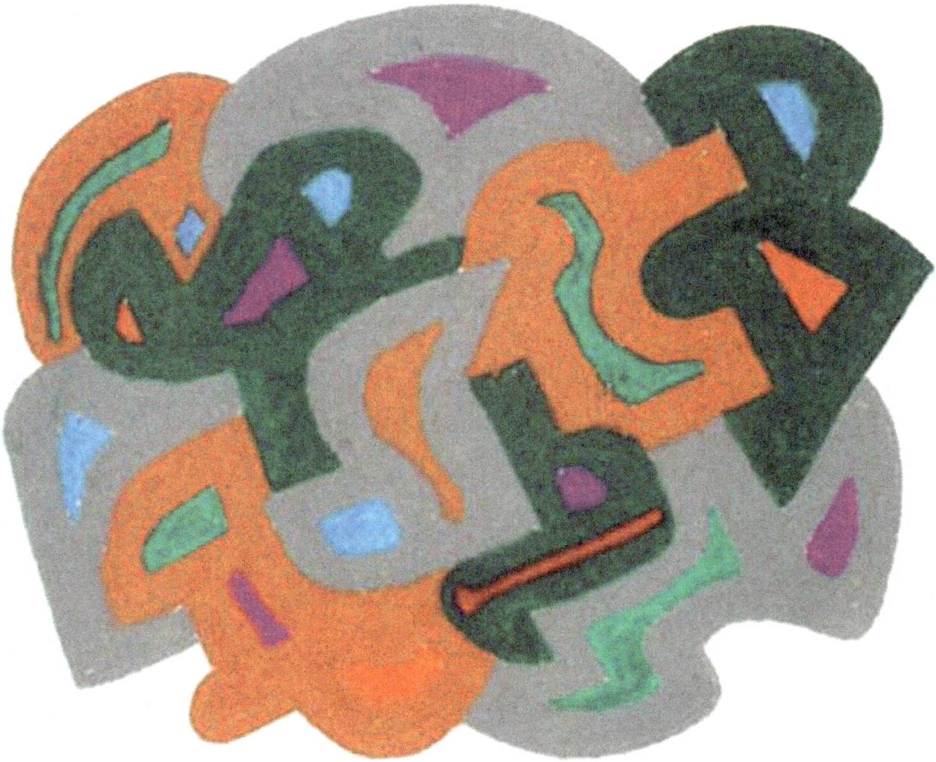

Eleven

THANK GOD FOR THE DOVE 6/78

Why should I,
when the wind blows high
and the beetle,
with steady stride,
crosses the lonely path.
For as he goes,
so go I.
And the black crow
sits on the pole
and laughs at me
and mocks me
and throws javelin spears

and insults and stones,
and jeers at me.
And over my shoulder,
I look at him
with jaundiced eye
and think, yes, I know,
you're here to stay,
but so is the dove.

LUCKY ONE   *6/78*

Now and again, the ...
but I don't mind.
And having smile,
the sun, the moon,
the mountains green,
the birds, the bee,
the cigarette tree
and the myriad
that cross my mind
with each second's look,
I do have ...
and am the lucky one,
when all is said and done.

DECISION TIME *6/78*

*F*low with me
fair flow pen.
   ...
When in the course ...
flowing as in a ...
and time will tell,
for time is,
and life is,
and people are,
and so am I.
And then that,
and the other,
and still another,
until the time of decision
descends like an ax
chopping the chord
and it is done
and shall not be redeemed,
for the decision has been made.
And what shall I do until then?
"Til that time
when snow falls softly
in central park
and men walk
hunched under snow-flakes,
content in their coats."
Then shall I ...
and the hearth fire
and the warm feet
and smiles in the stomach
and peace shall fall
like a welcome rain
in the slo-parched forest.

For this is!
And I am!
And shall be!

ONE MORE TIME 6/78

When I think of the ...
and all the ...
and think some more,
then I come upon ...
and the sun archs swiftly,
across the heavens,
about to set,
except for a few bright stars
that must be picked,
picked from a living sky
over rich, green grass
that flows and whispers
in the first fresh breaths
of the cool night air.
I long to be ...
and immerse myself in ...
and become
and enjoy
and flow with the sun
      the stars
      the grass
'ere I die.

I SHALL HAVE 6/78

*F*or even though I ...
and haven't,
yet I know I will
because the stream flows swiftly,
and I am its center.
It will take me
where it will go.
To still water,
deep beneath a rock,
to lap on desert shores,
to flow, fresh,
through green rushes,
(minnows between)
One day I will dry in a mud-hole
and my song will end,
but I shall grasp,
while I live,
and grasping,
have.

CLAIMING SPACES AGAIN 6/78

A note to ...
who shall read this and know
that it is I who shall prevail,
who shall win the chariot race,
whip in hand,

and it shall be me
who shall be acclaimed by me,
for I am my audience,
and I am my star,
and what I do
shall please myself,
for I am,
and shall be reckoned with,
who shall claim his space

SOME GREEN GRASS LEFT 6/78

Little do they ...
in the hearts of their ...
know of the ...
and what to do.
But I know, now,
and shall impart
the lucid contents
of a loving heart.
Charred sticks tumble
through burnt space.
Trees have their roots.
Rocks claim their place.
White dove knows,
but will not tell.
    Black crows jeer
    and tell me all.
The arching sun
has not quite set.
    The grass is green
    and not dead yet.

SCREW *6/78*

The screw,
wooden,
large threads,
used for courage
as in,
"Screw up your courage."
I did.
I twisted and turned,
tightened and wept,
twisted again,
'til exhausted and blistered,
I finally succeeded
in turning off love.
And so I have lived
with the pressure up high
and my valve,
through my effort,
has yet remained shut.
Now rusted and shut.
Not a trickle of love
has escaped,
have I loved.
And now, yet alive,
under the speeding arch,
sputtering arteries
splitting with strain,
valves of my heart
yielding in pain,
do I look for a way,
am desperate to know
how to loosen the screw,
how to open the gate,
let love flood out.
I know my mistake.

STONE

The stone
lies on the desert sand,
freckled, silver-gray,
with watermelon shape.
Quietly, heavily, it sits
with infinite patience,
through the long minutes,
hours, years of our lives,
absorbing suns rays,
stingingly hot on top,
cool below and dark.
And when the sun has set
and innumerable stars
claim the night sky
and the cool desert wind
whispers low on the sand,
the stone,
quietly radiates heat.
and living things
gather near
to receive the gift of warmth,
the energy from within.
The mother stone,
inscrutable, unfeeling,
yet not without feeling,
lies immobile, but alive,
steadfast, unfailing,
content in just being
the stone.

FOUR SYMBOLS 6/78

One

Great white dove
hangs in space
wings as large
as east to west
smiles at me,
at life, at death,
loving all,
with every breath.

Two

Black Crows
mock and jeer,
throw stones at me,
their yellow eyes,
swooping down,
call me names.
They glare and smirk
from the old dead tree.

Three

Charred stick figure
hurtles through space,
friend of the fire-wheel,
holocaust victim,
out of control.
Solidified dread.
Others follow,
equally dead.

Four

The tree, expanding,
grows upward and out,
filling the heavens
with awareness and life.
The roots below,
grow downward and out,
filling the earth
with awareness and life.

THE JOKE'S ON US **6/78**

When yellow dog's teeth
split iron rails
and lightning wracks the eye
and pines and willows
scream in the gale.
When the rain
splits the window pane
and enters like sperm
impregnating the unthinkable,
then shall blue faces
glow like ugly masks
in the black window
of eternal night
and slack-mouthed,
ragged-toothed,
evil laughter shall abound,
but emit no sound,

for the mask is mute,
and we are deaf,
and the joke is death,
and belongs on us.

ENOUGH 6/78

And why should I?
And why should you?
For I feel it is your right,
and my right too.
So don't feel badly.
It's not your fault.
Please do what you do,
and live how you live,
and reap what you sow.
And if that's enough for you,
it's enough for me, too.

THE OTHER SIDE 6/78

I have swum the river in the night,
and reached the other side.

I have a direction called *now*.
    When hungry, I eat.
    When tired, I sleep.
    When angry, I act out.
    When I love, I love.

I do what I do when I do.

I sensor not,
but let it flow,
for a look at truth
is both happy and bad,
and must be done
if I'm not to be sad.

THE CAT'S HOWL   *6/78*

The cat's howl
shattered peace
and silver bells
slipped to the ground.
(Belated rain from some lost cloud.)

Final rays
from a setting sun
burrowed deep
into thorny trees,
and crags,
undergrowth,
and black caverns.

Night fell
with the lynx
whose silent footfall,
and yellow eyes,
steady in the shadows,
stalked its prey.

TOO, TOO, DEEP, DEEP   6/78

When, in the light of the
too, too, deep, deep ...?
For then shall the mind
sharpen itself,
get to the point,
and thoughts would fly.
Sing out!
Be!
I take refuge,
and the deep, deep, too, too,
is within me,
yet will not speak.
Sometimes I'm unable
to find the proper channel,
the proper path toward the light.
Sometimes the desire is so strong
it cancels itself out,
and there is no flow,
only sensation,
motion and emotion.
When will the too, too, deep, deep
become a reality?

I think. I feel. I am.
But where is it?
I wish to see it.
Come to me.

FIRST STEP 6/78

*I*t was thus
that upon first seeing
that awesome starkness,
that looming side of the great blue whale,
those watery mud-plains slipping, vast,
into the ocean trench,
that *little-man*
should even attempt ...,
so on the brink,
so fearful the space,
so hopeful the spark,
the flickering candle,
hot in the dark
of the living breast,
that first step.

TIME TO BEGIN   *6/78*

For it is time,
and the execution
is all that remains,
for the energy converges,
and when it is done,
then shall the ripping-point
be fire hardened
and ready to work
upon life and the world.

FREEDOM   *6/78*

The rent and tattered heart
shall mend itself anew,
beat with purpose,
 tight-knit,
 blood-red
fine-textured and strong.
Shall beat a new pathway
 through greenness,
 tree trunks,
 foliage and blackness,
 stars and cumulous,
and shall be as the air,
 rippling, swift,
 low on high grass,
free.

SAMENESS

That this too, too,
in the infinite,
speeding universe,
infiltrating all
and the space in between,
black and cold,
that we,
lost in this infinite,
roam toward,
or away from,
but always speeding,
yet in divine rhythm,
flowing, pulsing
as a bright heart beats with love,
excitement,
enthusiasm,
lusting for life
and the peculiarity
that this,
and the infinitely expanding stars
and the blackness
and separateness
and the close beat of the heart
are one and the same.

I KNOW ME 6/78

*U*p from the stomach
let it emerge.
   I think hard,
     but see gray nothing,
     yet feel intensely.
I shall be pliant,
     patient,
     nurturing.
I live inside,
and it tells me what,
   but not in words.
Its messages come,
   jackal in sheep's disguise,
   dark clouds hiding sunny skys.
Nevertheless,
   I will decipher,
   for I know me,
even if I don't.

MOON-SHATTERED 6/78
(Automatic writing poem)

*M*oon - shattered in three.
Grass shadows lay wrinkled
   on midnight sand.
Wolves howl in forgotten woods.
   When will the ...

have mercy on me.
April is the violet month.
March is the violent month.
The man with the coat
   had no face.
Love becomes the little child.
Shall I win my race?
She whispered in the hall.
Highway noises and crickets.
I may be late,
   save me a ticket.
She flickered an eyelid
   and stuttered.
No one knows me,
   not even myself.
Cat's tail hangs
   on the lone pine tree.
April is the month of promise.
Rain has no peer.
My father is dead,
   but not in my heart.
I'll love when I do,
   or I won't.
Stay with me, fair one.
I know her,
   but she doesn't know me.
Race car drivers
   never drink beer.
I know my place,
   but I'm not there.
When will the yellow flower
   dip it's head and drink water?
Train whistles
   frighten the night.
Where do beetles go to sleep?
Roots join hands,
   bow their heads,

   and pray.
I'll be a tree
   instead of a me.
She sang a midnight song
   then gave it to me,
free.

WHERE SHALL I GO?   *6/78*

*H*oney rays pouring,
   flowing thickly
   over the brim.
And where shall a poor mind go
   when there is no thought?
Wind scatters to sea.
Stones lies on sand.
For I am the only one.
And I am the lonely one.
   Cat sleeps in grass.
   Moon sleeps in sky.
Where shall I go,
   if I'm not with me?

Random Thoughts

Myself
takes up a lot of my time.

Psychology

Psychology is the tool with which
we change the flat tire of the mind.

Knowledge

Knowledge of death
puts a *"zinger"*
in the drink of life.

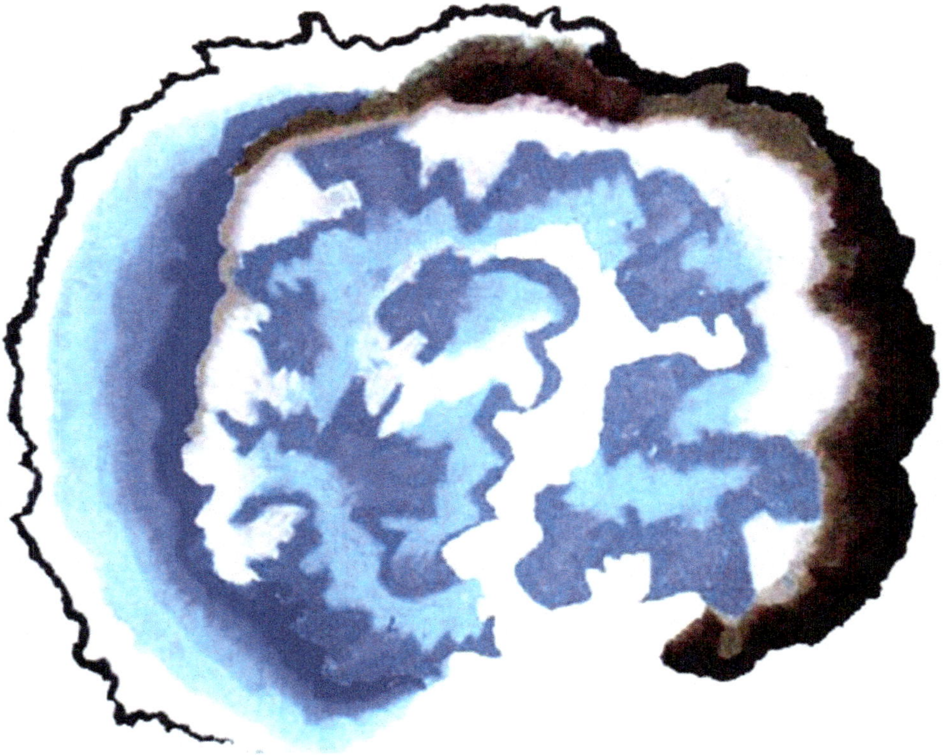

Twelve

SOMETHING MEANINGFUL *6/78*

*F*or he both ...
 in the last analysis,
 having looked for
 and found ...
Then, upon his first seeing,
 laid the groundwork.
And it was thus that beginnings began.
Slowly at first,
 the dawning,
but clearer and ever more distinct,
 the ... around him became ...
Until that first time

    when the amorphous
       began taking shape,
indistinct, at first,
       but forming into an unmistakable ...
Which led to solidarity
       and oneness.
A foundation
       for the first time solid,
       upon which to build
something meaningful,
something lasting.

ANGELS SING SWEET SONGS   ***6/78***
(Automatic writing poem)

First me, then we.
This path will do.
In the mist and clearing,
    the dead branch silhouette.
Everywhere the song.
Night-birds cry,
    then spin their heads.

First the thunder,
    then the rain.

Closed eyelids, smoothed brow.
My heart shows teeth
    in a smile.
I love to love.

Fourteen hundred elephants
    and not a blade of grass.
The willow tree
    swayed in the breeze.
Yellow dogfish,
    bright black eyes.
Ripples and swirls
    in still water.
Frogs swim under,
    webbed feet trailing.
I drink with my eyes.
White clouds, blue sky,
    reflected in still water.
Seaweed holds water
    so it cannot move.
Angels sing sweet songs.

THE HEARTSORE   6/78

And once dragged from its hiding place,
    we see its countenance, weak, slithery,
    frightened of the bright lights,
    fearful, ugly in the sun,
    out of place and unable to return.
What shall we do with it?
What will it do by itself?
It is lost. It is big.
It needs care and feeding.
It seems to have weight and mass,
    but no sense about how to cope.
It must be dried, spoon-fed and taught.

It must come to be tanned by the sun.
It must develop calluses by working.
Its eyes are watery
    and its vision is distorted.
We must dry it's eyes
    so that it can see clearly.
We have to work the fat off it
    to see if it can be a something.
It is ugly in its rebirth,
    but we don't know what it is yet.
It must use itself to see what it will be.
It leaves spots on the pavement.
It is big and unused.
It seems to have potential,
    just looking at it,
    but until it does something,
    we will not know just how much.
A lot of effort must be expended,
    especially, at first.

ART   *6/78*

Whatever comes out,
    when it comes out,
    is meaningful,
    and has its place,
    whether mundane, boring,
    trite or uninteresting,
    whether exciting,
    filled with insight,
    philosophy, beauty or love.

It is also particular
    upon the face of this earth,
    because it could not have been said,
    or made, or have come about
    by any other human
    in the same way,
    or in the same year, month or day,
    or with the same words,
    or with the same overtones of feeling,
    or with the same connotations.
Therefore, everything is valuable that comes out,
    and is meaningful to someone.

Even if it is nothing,
    it is something.

Even if it is something to withhold,
    or something to shout about,
    or something to rework,
    it has its place,
    and should be given its due,
    and respected,
    and acknowledged
    for what it is,
    whatever it is.
For, it cannot be repeated,
    even by the same individual,
    and only comes out once
    during a passing moment of time,
    and is entirely unique.

Therefore, whatever comes out
    is an expression of male
    or female,
    and being human-made,
    and not nature-made,
    is art.

BLUE, THE GRASS OF THE HAPPIER HEART   7/78

Blue is the grass
   of the happier heart,
   but shall not grow
   where charred trunks
   stab a hopeless sky
   and black-sand desert reaches,
   and pavement lines converge.
There, rocks pray
   to superheated air
   and die inside.
There, the sun hangs limp
   and shall not be revived.
There, just my heart
   and a tiny fish,
     content in it's bowl,
     have lived and loved,
survived.

RAIN, WHERE ARE YOU?   7/78

Rain, where are you?
I need you now.
I need to feel your cool breeze
   blowing up from the west.
I need to feel the dampness
   in your air.
I need to see you light

the warm night sky,
and hear your approaching rumblings.
When will you come?

THE THOUGHT 7/78

The thought
   strikes me full
   like some silver ray
   from a mighty star.

It pierces my mind
   and bursts,
   flooding the interior
   with bright, white light.
I have a new perspective.

The thought,
   comes swinging through
   like some mighty ax
   with gleaming blade.

It strikes the trunk
   and fells the tree,
   and I know that my lost ...
   is well fed,
ready for caring and love.

The thought,
   wells up
   from my entrails,

becomes one
with mind and spirit.

It sits, shining,
    on my shoulder
    like *Lili's* silver bird
    and sings *(golden trumpets)*
    musical truths,
glorious, in my ear.

The thought,
    when I relax,
    pours out golden,
    honey-rays,
    brimming, spilling,
    letting me know
    that I am ...,
    and certainty
    sits within me,
    a strong foundation
for action.

The thought
    I work.

I wait.

WHEN SHALL THE ...

(Part 1)
When shall the ...?
And in the morning go ...?
And then shall that change anything?
And when shall I ...?
For she said she would,
    but didn't.
And I am bitter
    and shall not be contented,
    for it is my life,
    and I'm the one who pays.
Lost in the river of life,
    through dark forests I go,
    wondering about the light,
    listening for rain and distant thunder.
For rain shall save me,
    lightly pattering on thick leaves,
    it comes whispering
    with the cool breeze.
Then increasing in tempo,
    and soon is upon us,
    and we are the heart of the cloudburst,
    and our faces are drenched,
    as we lift them,
    and taste the cool rain water,
    and our dry lips are soothed.
The wrinkled brow eases,
    and a smile warms our faces,
    having grown from the inside.
For peace is upon us,
    and we deserve it,
    for we have traveled far,
    and will not go that way again.

7/78

But now is the time for reflecting,
    and as the rain lessens,
    so our contented,
    peaceful feelings
    turn to thoughtfulness,
    and we proceed, as before,
    down the same trodden pathway,
    hopeful and with renewed strength,
    and new spirit,
    and new step,
    and the forests change to meadows
    with wild flowers
    and crystal rivulets
    winding their unhurried way
    to the larger brooks,
    and we begin our exciting journey
    in earnest.
For we have a new bearing,
    a new essence,
    a new calling,
    and it will enrich our lives,
    and we will grow and sing,
    and draw and write,
    and make things we want to make.
The most important being
    the making of ourselves,
    for this shall be the richest work,
    the most rewarding work
    the most meaningful
    and fulfilling work we can do.
The journey could take us
    to the land of blue sky *(top)*
    and green grass *(bottom)*
    and nothing else.
Just sky and grass,
    blue and green,

clean and fresh,
invading our senses.
We could go to purple mountains
against an orange sky
with a red warlord sun
about to set.
We may see silver clouds
in fish forms
gleaming in airy heavens,
or one lone star, venus,
bright against the midnight blue
of a tranquil sky.
Under the ground, could we go,
through serpentine tunnels,
deep in the earth,
where we find treasures
rich beyond dreams,
diamonds, emeralds,
friendships, loves,
or over the falls,
falling free for miles,
and entering cool, green water.
Plunging deeply,
through ever greener,
ever darker colors and pressures,
with silver bubbles
clustering about us
and suspended.
Then effortlessly rising,
plenty of breath,
we enjoy our ascending.
Up from the dark green coolness
rising with bubbles
to the silvery surface,
undulating, mirroring above,
and as we break through the surface
into raw sunlight,

green trees,
massive rocks, foliage,
and a fresh strong breeze,
we know that this is where we belong,
and everything feels right,
and connected,
and that we have achieved our final
completeness.
Lifting from the waters surface,
we might float
like a bubble,
lightly born on the air,
and drift out of the canyon,
steep slopes descending,
over roads and pathways,
over the snake-like silvery river,
over the winding highways
and traveling cars,
and clouds,
and sun,
immersed in the breeze and blue sky.
Over the villages, towns, cities
of our birth,
we get the wide view,
the panorama of this green earth,
from which we have been born.
We understand
by our underview,
and our overview,
that this is truly where we live.
That none can take it from us.
And that it is good.
We welcome it,
for it is beautiful,
and we see it from the overview
and the under-view,
and we claim it ours,

and it claims us for its own,
and we are inseparable,
its follies, our follies,
its joys, our joys,
for it is,
and we are,
and we are it,
and it is us,
and to hurt a part of it
is to hurt each of us,
and to love it,
is to be loved by it.
And we must not forget the intimate things.
The beetles, hurriedly
   crossing the pathways.
Spring green grass shoots.
Bees, struggling
   to find a way out
   through a partially closed window,
   not seeing the opening.
The silent worm,
   content in its bed of warm earth,
   and our intimate daily relations,
   our lovingness,
   our angry-ness,
   our unfulfilled-ness,
   our hopefulness,
   and the knowledge that,
   though we are all together,
   yet, each is alone.
That we can never know, fully,
   what another feels,
   for there are no rules,
   and there is no right or wrong,
   only ebbing and flowing.
I give way to your push,
   you yield to my advance.

And this is the way
    toward true satisfaction
    and fulfillment,
    and happiness,
    in this rich time of our life.
For when two yield
    or push at the same time,
    there is no motion.
But the ebb and the flow,
    the pushing and yielding,
    this makes for motion
    and excitement,
    and getting things done
    in a loving and expressive way.
For by yielding,
    we acknowledge the other
    in his or her pushing,
    and in sensing the other's yield,
    we are aware of our own
    unmistakable affect.
And so, to ebb and flow,
    this is the way to go.

WHEN SHALL THE ...

(Part 2)
Moon tilts head and sings.
Frog croaks in lonely grass.
I look up from my cup and sigh.
The sun hangs limp from the humid day.
A blind man taps the sweltering pavement

    and thinks of an August moon.
For I have never ...
    but I desperately want ...
"This is the time."
    said the midnight sun.
"Where shall we go?"
This, from the goat.
Water runs in circles down the pane.
I called to my ...
    she did not hear,
    but continued sewing.
Yellow roses,
    content in high green grass.
The snow fell, silvery,
    against the shining night.
How will the ...
    when it wants to ...
    know when to ...
The big-horn knows
    and so does the crow
    and the frozen apple orchard
    and the colored neon lights
    of barrel house street signs.
Lifting her glass, she smiled and said ...
I dropped my gaze to my plate
    and fingered my teacup.
For you said you would...
    and I, with glistening eyes,
    saw your shining form
    and believed
    with all the truth in my heart,
    that ...
But now, after the snowfall,
    when things are white-buried
    in perfect light,
I watch the mountain move to the west,
    and the clouds riveted to the blue,

and ask myself. How could I ...
    after all these years ...
    come to such a ...
And so, the decision must be made,
    and hangs upside down on my soul,
    and waits in the wings,
    for now it is time to perform.
And what will I say
    when the footlights are high
    and the band begins
    and the thousand audience eyes
    with the energy of heartbeats
    pierces my form?
What shall I tell them?
Shall I say ...
    "I lost my little boy!"
    and sink to my knees,
    head in arms and crying?
Shall I be pitied then?
Shall they not say,
    "Stand like a man!
    Show your strong arm!
    Thrust your jaw!"
Is what they see, me?
Is what I see, me?
Are they, they?
The cow-bell clanks its way to the barn.
The boy and girl huddle close in the car.
The maple trees that line the streets
    are wet in the rain
    and maple seeds squirm like worms
    on sidewalks
    and clipped green lawn.
I know a fish with a silver side.
I know a buzzard with a black under-wing
    and a short red head.
I know that sleep heals the soul

       as well as the body.
The time shall come,
       is coming now,
       and shall not be denied.
"Hasten the fact!" he cried.

WHEN SHALL THE ...

(Part 3)
*F*or in the beginning there was ...
And this is the beginning now.
And all that was, is the beginning ...
       and ending.
For beginning and ending
       run a parallel course,
       and it shall not be me
       who'll ask for a change.
I like it, thus.
Nor shall I despair,
       since, if there is always beginning,
       there is always hope.
And I am joyful at ending.

For I welcome the ending
       as I do the beginning,
       though they are often intertwined
       as two vines slipping apart.
I may have beginning and ending
       simultaneously for a while.
Yet time shall separate the two,
       only to involve them again.

FEAR DREAM 78

*T*he wind carried me aloft.
I clung to a large yellow bag.
My friend grasped his umbrella
    at the bottom of the hill.
It became a light metal frame,
    and caught the gusting wind.
Up he went, almost aloft,
    skittering up the hill,
    legs clipping the tops
    of tall green grass.
He reached the knoll and fell,
    sprawling and falling
    over the dry grass slope,
    until the hill broke away,
    and he rode the crumbling earth
    as he would an ocean breaker,
    head protruding.
The earth-wave broke
    and swallowed him.
If I could not save him
    he would be buried.
I ran to the mounding pile
    of still earth.
Where shall I dig?
How would I feel
    in the heavy blackness
    unable to breathe?

7/78

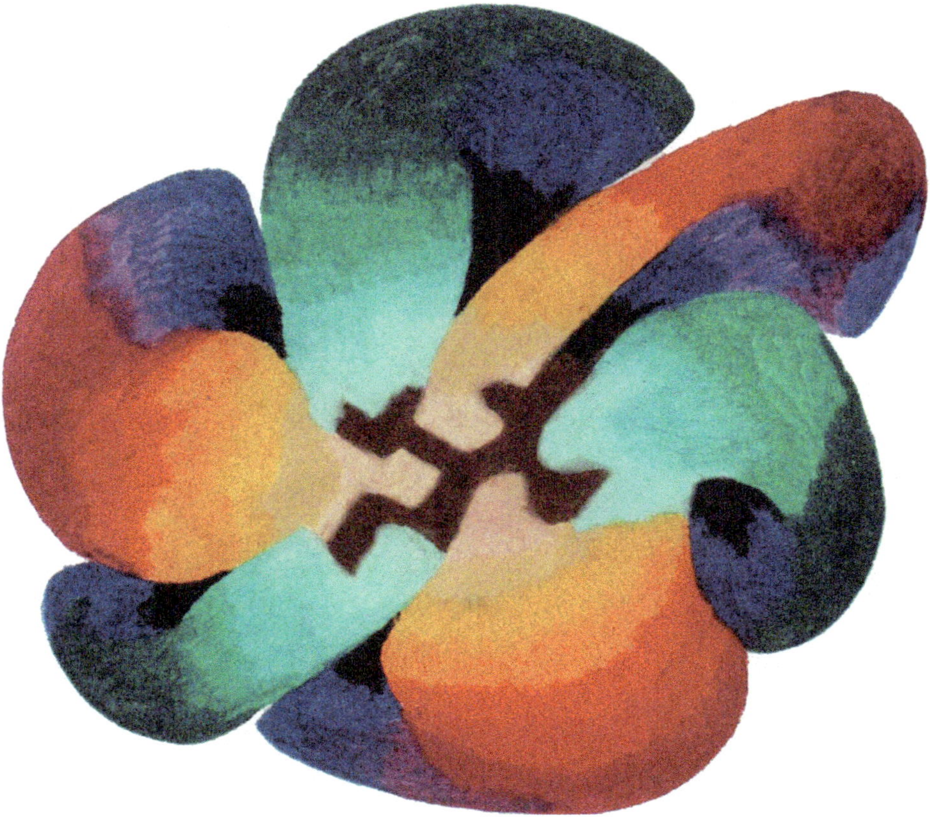

Thirteen

WHAT SHE SAID   7/78

(Part 1)
She said to me ...
    and the buried light appeared,
    came swinging in the attic
    of lost memory
    and illumined, brilliant,
    that one lost instant when,
    transformed from boy to ghost,
    I saw that tortured face.
It came, the light, on a sweltering hand,
    and showed me the way.
Shall I have the courage to see?
Can I gaze on that lost face?

Those wrinkled lines around the eyes?
That wistful smile
   that held me close?
Those eyes that claimed me,
   "Mine, for all time!?"
For she would never let me down,
   but would rather lose her life.
I loved her so,
   and told her so
     with golden rays of light
     gleaming from my eyes
     as she held me close.
And then the picture darkened,
   faded from my view,
   by one last remark,
   one last glance,
   some last gesture
   taken heavily.
   It came ... my loss.
Or was it insidious?
Did it creep and steal
   upon my back
   from the darkness
   of my time with her,
   after ...?
Until without warning,
   I knew the door had closed,
   never to be reopened.
Perhaps, now,
   "like sight, once lost,
   regained for just an instant,
   and then forever gone",
   I hope.
I loved her so,
   and she, me,
   and would read me stories,
   and I would journey with her

through many a golden land
of love.
And we were one,
 and basked in each other's aura,
 and strode down golden trails
 strewn with poetry
 and adventure.

I loved her so,
 and she, me.

Until the specter appeared!
In what strange shape?
Was it my blond-haired brother
 with innocent eyes
 and lashes, long and dark,
 that beguiled my
dear one away?
Was it *he* that diverted
 our way of being?
Sent me on the course
 of slithering monsters
 with swollen eyes.
Was it *he* that set me adrift
 (unknowingly) a fool
 on the high seas of life?
Was it *he* that sent me
 stupidly on my way,
to bumble in doorsteps,
 beg for a pittance,
 thank the whip
 for the lash,
 or fitfully doze
 these forty years?
I think so,
 but will never know.

(Part 2)
*D*im lights in dark doorways.
Silently the rat rustles the scraps.
I love the golden eyes of eagles.
Clouds drift and dream of rain and sun.
Little does the ...
    in the heart of the ...
    know that ...
What a surprise,
    her white thighs.
She told me I shouldn't,
    and lowered her eyes.
Her footfall came with the wind.
I reached for the knob on the door.
I loved her thighs
    as I loved the moon.
We knew ...
    But we don't ...
But we can ...
    I love you lizard.
Beetles strike out with decision.
Tools are built with precision,
    and so is mine.

MOON-TEARS   *7/78*

*I*nto the boiling pit I'm thrown.
The full moon cries high in the sky.
Tears speed downward.

If I, in anguish, survive that saturated night,
    shall I finally see that rising sun,

with streaming rays,
light the forest of my lost dreams?

Shall I finally walk, proud and free,
    among its leaves,
    and leaf-strewn pathways,
    a primitive,
    acting and reacting,
    enjoying and loving?

And shall I see a midday, a sunset, a clear night
    with cold stars, gleaming in their places?
Shall I be awestruck at their magnificence as I stand,
    secure, at last, in my own jungle?

I shall do my work!

ALIVE HE GOES, INTO THE COFFIN   7/78
(Automatic writing poem)

*H*e sold her down the river.
I loved to touch her ...
She used to snuggle close,
    but doesn't anymore.
I loved her thigh above her stocking.
Her tongue struck lightning to my ...
I loved to love her love.
Eager was the hasty heart.
She shimmied on the floor.
The eyes of friends were lusting.
My bleeding heart was sore.

She took me up the ladder,
    led me by the nose,
    and let me put my burning hand
    above her silky hose.
I sold her down the river.
There's anguish in my heart.
My fat and watery eyesore crying evermore.
What did I do to give her away
    in those early days of my lost love?
Her heart was bright,
    and her love was true.
She wrote me letters.
I wrote, too.
The boys at the party lapped her up.
I lay bleeding on the stair,
my fat and watery eyesore
    exposed for all to see.
I dammed my feelings,
    corked them tight,
    decided to <u>break</u> my little boy.
I put him screaming, alive,
    into the coffin,
    and swallowed my soul.

THE FOREST HOLDS THE ANSWER   7/78
(Automatic writing poem)

Marriage is a fake.
Trees, still, on the prairie.
She bundled up her skirt.
I wait and waiting, wait.
She locked the door and locked her ...

Refrigerators never close.
This car needs gas.
Oranges are ripe after seven.
The bedclothes tell a tale.
Two bright shoes.
I love her walking pattern.
"April is in My Mistress' Face,"
    but in her heart, a cold September.
They both were fish-mongers.
I eat my peach, then toss the pit.
Summer spells trouble.
The tug of the silken cord.
To cut my cord
    is to cut my life.
Lying adrift, he goes with the tide.
Anguish strikes his face.
He whispers to God,
    who does not hear,
    so empty is his space.
When will the silk cord break?
I see him drifting out to sea,
    returning to some lost friend.
He shall live his life
    and shall not sell another
    down the river.
Come to grips with a roving bear.
She lighted thirteen candles.
The smoke of the fire eternally present.
I leapt and leaping free ...
Put the candle on the table.

HE PUT ME ON THE HOSE
(Automatic writing poem)

Yellow spades the natural night.
It must have been a truly horrendous region.
All he recalls is the wing and the air.
For he was the only one,
    and he was the lonely one.
You ought to go to bed with him.
Spaced out, he rides the yellow tide.
Joy was in his heart
    and incredible strength was in his arms.
He brimmed like a sated monkey.
April is in the hasty heart.
You ought to go to bed with him
    and dream awhile tonight.
I bit the net which hurt my teeth.
He rose to the never-never land,
    and hit the painful mark.
I think I'll go to bed with him
    and dream awhile tonight.
Needles and drugs enter my arms.
I cry like a long lost baby.
I don't want to do it,
    but I love him very much.
In the middle of the night
    he caught the fingers of my hair.
Around his yellow hair
    he tied a yellow ribbon.
Around his head he wore a yellow ribbon.
He wore it in the evening
    when the ice was on the ground.
He wore it in the morning
    and his heart was very gay.
I know a bee who may sting me.
Into the fire he goes with his clothes.

Painfully, I bite my toes,
    and smell the evening as it goes.
Daddy was a giant bear.
He put me on the hose.

HASTY HEART 7/78
(Automatic writing poem)

When will the hasty heart come to it's senses?   1
I know a picture that won't hang straight.   2
When in the light of the her
    will I begin to attack the now?   3
April is in my mistress' face,
    but in her heart, a cold September.   4
Oranges hang high in the old Oak tree.   5
I begin to worry on the wire in the sky.   6
The beetle walks briskly across the pathway.   7
I know a needle who doesn't like me.   8
All the king's horses and all the king's men
    couldn't put Humpty together again.   9
He tried with a wooden paddle.   10
Gracefully the canoe would glide.   11
I have a wish instead of a dish.   12
Give me some soap and I'll soap your ear.   13
He riveted the boiler plate.   14
The farmer takes a wife.   15
The wife climbs out on the limb.   16
The limb is holding strong.   17
The tree is rooted, firm   18
When will the singing tree sing it's song?
When will the moon open it's eyes?
Gray clouds pass while pale moon sleeps.
In the winter, the song of the tale.

I know the bartered bride.
April is in her face.
I know a tattered bride.
Her heart is in her mouth.
She hangs, suspended, waiting.
When will the fine cord break?
Into what sweet bed shall she fall?
Will she break on icy rocks?
I think I'll go to bed and dream a while tonight.

PARTIAL INTERPRETATION – HASTY HEART 7/78
(Line by line)

1   When shall I feel confident to act with assurance?
2   I cannot get my family life to operate correctly.
3   When will I attack my problems with assurance?
4   My wife smiles and promises, but doesn't deliver.
5   Good things will happen if I can gain assurance.
6   I worry about my position and upcoming decisions.
7   I have enough life in me. Correct decisions are possible.
8   I am hampered by my early traumas.
9   I tried for many years, ineffectively, to make things work.
10 A given: impossible to make unaware mate understand.
11 My <u>dream</u> of what I could have – but not <u>reality</u>.
12 I have a wish, not an actuality.
13 With personal power, I could clean up the mess.
14 I know I can do tough things successfully.
15 Naive, I got married and worked hard for success.
16 I am forced to maintain this ever-more unbalanced state.
17 I'm tired of trying to balance the act.
18 I am strong but with sufficient loads will break.

LOVED LAND 7/78

Summer weeds delight the eye.
The elm tree sways and purrs.
Cherry blossoms sing in sweet surrender.

I dig the digging clay.
I climb the singing tree.
I bloom, my heart, as the orchard.

Sun and wind, thick like snow.
Quietly I sit between
    and watch the panoramic games;
    "heat lightning."

Thunder rolls in rhythmic wonder.
Lightly rest my eyelids
    in the middle of the rain.
Moon and stars,
    mirror in the magic mind.
I bask in the love of a sweetened heart.
I eat the peach of contented time.

THE SMILING EYE 7/78
(Automatic writing poem)

I love to be kissed by a smiling eye.
    Here we go with winter.
Long legs and silky thighs.

The butter on the bread, he cried.
I love her in the large print dress.
    She walks with stylistic grace,
    serenity in her face.
Lovely lasses wear dark glasses.
    Cotton candy is fine and dandy.
A punch in the nose will do just fine.
    She runs the gamut, tip to toe.
Ice cold rivers give me shivers.
    I don't think I want to play.
Iron maidens in the surf.
    She lifted an elegant eye.
She slipped by the table and fell.
    I love to feel her delicate feet.
When shall the moon open its eyes?
    Clouds in the sky marked in gray.
Needles and bushes make glorious sounds.
    I kissed her nose and fingered her toes.
She always makes a mortal cry.
    I like the salt-lick lips.
A belt in the front and a bow in the back.
    I'm willing to try anything once.
Where do pigeons fly,
    when they fly away from me?
She stuffed a pillow in the fire.
    Give me some time and I'll work things out.
April is in my heart along with purple and black.
    Her eyes have seen the devil, undisguised.
How shall I make it over the years?
    Feet tread softly on the earth.
The blanket is a mystery.
    She howls at the moon and cries.
Night is a thing of the past,
    but also is present.
She loves her little whipping girl.
    Bones and tears are part of the bride.
She said she wouldn't go on.

    Her waist is in terrible taste.
Her tits and her ass are ready for mass.
    April is in her heart as well as her face.
She leaves with nary a trace.
    I love the bubbles in her heart.
This punching bag is soft.
    This punching bag has weight and mass
    as well as ass.
What shall we do with this?
    The bird and the bear make quite a pair.
If you call me a taxi, I'll call you one, too.
    Honesty is sometimes brutal.
Do we have the right?
    How far can you stretch?
Can I stretch with you?
    Eager is the smiling face.
Compliant is the heart.
    I close no open door,
    but go before the cart.

THE WEEPING WILLOW AND THE BUSH   7/78

Why should I,
    when the ...
    is in the morning.
The sun is shining high
    in a blue and yellow sky.
For, if I do,
    what will I gain?
Clouds are rising swiftly
    to black space of night.

The willow said to the bush,
    "I like you, but you're crowding me."
I need to swing my sweeping branches,
    feel the wind and sway.
They must swing free,
    if I'm to be me.
I recognize your right.
    (Your bundle is tight,
    but not impossibly so.)
Stay for the race,
    but give me some space.
The bush and the tree
    are permanent friends.
They live side by side
    near the fast flowing river.
On grassy cut banks
    they're warmed by the sun,
    cooled by an afternoon breeze.
Occasionally they held hands.
Warm hearts connect them.
They know their places,
    and they are there.
The tree needs room,
    but not too much.
(They love to touch)

GIVE ME A BREAK   7/78
(Automatic writing poem.)

April is the month of mating.
Silently, in groups of three,

the stars appear,
awakened for the dance.
I live with one lost love.
Marry is the month of May.
I live for Shining-Big-Sea-Water.
The crow in the street
   turned his head
   and looked at me.
When, in the light of ...
   shall the ...
   and then begin?
Mother was a proper maiden.
Father was a pill.
I like chocolate,
   but it doesn't like me.
The truck hit the boy and ran.
Flowers live a dirty life.
I knew a kitten
   who had only one mitten.
Sorrow sears my soul.
Fourteen hundred elephants
   trampled down the grass.
Irrevocable is your own sweet smile.
Give me a dollar for that blue cheese.
Nothing is a simple state.
Marge will marry me,
   and I shall care for her.
We only think twice,
   and then we throw up.
Can't you see this little me?
I want love as I want cherries.
Songs shall dwell in my heart.
Race car drivers hit the wall
   and die.
The horse and the cart
   is my story.
Girl of the Limberlost,

show me the way.
Trees of the summer night
   twist on their trunks.
For she is the live one,
   and she is the right one,
   and if I'm in love,
   she'll give me away.
Water wrings an empty heart.
Fish sing in bowls.
I like a trumpet,
   as well as a strumpet.
The hardened heart
   beats like wood.
Up from the stomach,
   I bellow.
This dream provides a scheme.
I live with one lost memory.
I yield to my mistake.
Come on, dad,
   give me a break.

THE GERRARD HOUSE TRIP   7/78
(Automatic writing poem)

I think I'll go to sleep a while.
Midnight noises make such awful sounds.
I wish I were a tree instead of a me.
I like to think of April in the spring.
"Throw me a bone," said the dog.
April is in my mistress' face.
Sing a song of sixpence.

Four and twenty blackbirds
 baked in to a pie.
Elephants weave funny trails in the garden.
High and low the well-spring goes.
Give me the son.
I will weave a pattern when I go.
Early worship days.
Dairy maids will grow.
 (All in a row.)
I will walk to Daddy.
S-u-m-m-er-time and the livin' is easy.
David was born late in March.
When will the plant come in? Today?
I love to lift a cuddly thing.
Hi Ho the dairy – O,
 the farmer takes a wife.
I want a fish instead of a wish.
The merry month of May.
Our hearts were young and gay,
 as in the morning.
The wife gets the son.
I wish he'd go away.

GORILLA DREAM   *8/78*
(Automatic writing poem)

*Y*ellow was the hasty heart.
I loved her in the morning
 when the dew was on the ground.
I remember mamma in the spring.
How does this thing figure?

The yellow rose has no hose.
Theoretically, time will tell.
Hello, dolly, what's in it for you?
Along came a blackbird
    and snipped off her nose.
Fourteen hundred elephants
    trampled down the grass.
A truly devastating region.
All clear on the Western Front.
I'm free, cried Sally.
Easter eggs make lots of sense.
I want a banana for my very own.
She peeled me a grape.
Daddy was a rouser.
Simple Simon met a Pie-man.
April is in my mistress' face,
    but in her heart, a cold September.
I want mamma,
but she doesn't want me.

SHOWER DREAM   8/78
(Automatic writing poem)

Now, in the dawn of the new day.
April is gone from my mistress' face.
And in her heart is nothing.
I have come to the vantage point.
Silence is in my body.
Where have you gone, sweet birds?
I love life with a twist.
"Isn't that so?" said the crow.
Hallelulja! I'm a bum!

Snow falls in South Nantucket.
When will the ...?
Ice is on the window pane.
Hello, dolly, what's your story?
See the animal twist and writhe.
How are little toys made?
I remember mamma in the spring.
After-shocks are shocking.
His brain whirled
    like an egg-beater in Hades.
See here, Mister! I love, too!
The Jack-in-the-Box knows.
He loved his fingers and toes.
Life is lonely as it goes.
Where does Harriet figure in all this?
Fourteen hundred elephants
    tiptoe on the grass.
Let me have that fly swatter.
I can take care of myself.
But what about all these people?
Serrania loves the dog.
The dog is in the kitchen.
So is the cat.
Hello, dolly, what's your name?
Give me some skin, pal.
I know you,
    but you don't know me.
Time will wear an even rug.
Simple Simon met a Pieman
    going to the fair.
Said Simple Simon
    to the Pieman,
"Let me taste your ware."
The idyllic flower bloomed.
Hello, Guy, what's your story?
The Goodyear Blimp floats high.
Sometimes I think of Mamma.

Now is the time for sun.
Give me some skin.
Sometimes the burner is high.
Swing high, swing low,
    sweet chariot.
Comin' for to carry me home.
   (Rest of Song)

IN THE BRITTLE EVENING   *8/78*

*I*n the brittle evening
    oranges hang high
      on one strong tree.
I kiss the air
    and see it flowing.
I breathe the gleaming blossoms.
I feel the earth's weight
    as my own, warm.
The damp, black earth
    pressing on my feet.
I grow from earth
    and have the right,
      as any plant,
        to bloom.

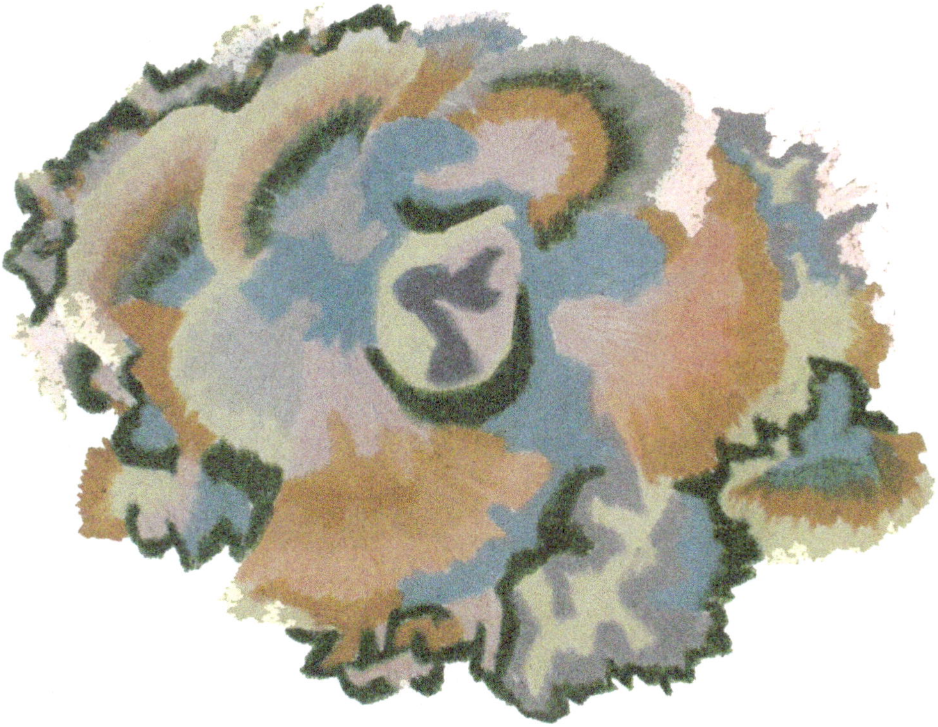

Fourteen

THE BURNING TREE *9/78*

I would the burning tree
 ask it's question.
For, in the evening,
 starlight whispers, softly.
Calls to me in pussy-willow tones
 that reach my middle mind
 and blow cool zephyrs
 across the shallows of my heart.
I know you, mind.
And you, feather-softened thoughts
 that yield not,
 but as the stone,

press their burning way.
Come to me sweet one.
You, with smiling eye.
Linger softly in my soul
    and cover me with lemon-love.
    for, I do.

SHADOW DANCE   *2/79*

Now the shadows
begin their dance
on walls of silence.
And flowers bloom
where once the driven sand
lay barren.
I know the heart
in all it's beating,
and blood,
well driven,
sounding on the temple's shores.
Little did the cavern
know of morning light.
Little did the seed
anticipate the rain.
I see you, little boy.
Smile in the face of tears long shed.
Hit me little one,
I deserve your blow.
Hit me, hit me.
I love you so.

THE YOUNG MAN'S FANCY   *4/79*

*F*or in the evening,
the young man's fancy
<u>does</u> turn to thoughts of love.
And this young butterfly
shall be denied no more.
Nor shall the willow
springing from the river bottom.
I know you, soul.
You want red meat
and green things to eat.
Dead men speak no more.
The stone sits, heavy,
on the desert floor.
Without growth,
only death remains.
Be near, sweet spirit.
I breathe your fragrance.
I hold you to me
like a mother does, her baby.
I clasp you to my breast,
like a brother home from war.
I am not lonely,
nor shall I be again.
I have you, my soul,
for my friend.

WHERE SHALL YOU GO? *4/79*

*W*here shall you go,
sweet hopes for a loving life?
Where shall life take you, now?
Into the world to work your way?
To this attraction, then that?
And finally resolve on some special one?
And, what about me?
Shall I die a thousand deaths?
Shall I mourn through my last hour?
Shall you be some spent pit
aching in my heart?
I suspect you will.
I lament that which cannot be resolved.
Where shall you go?
Where shall I go,
now that we are truly
finished?

WORK TO DO *4/79*

*I*t is I who am I.
There - are you!
Thank me, fine friend,
    for the distinction.
Kill that tomato!
Up from the darkness
    of whole existence,

she waddled toward the toilet.
I heard her scream when she landed.
There was no time for blackberry pie.
I wanted to listen,
    but she would not share.
I set the trap,
    then ran for my life.
My face was gaunt,
    but my arms were full.
She wouldn't listen,
    so I shouted,
    "Come here, baby,
    or we're through!"
I heard the sobbing in the night.
It carried for miles.
    "What do you mean, duty?"
I lifted the lid and looked,
then into the maelstrom,
I leapt, with a fury.
    "I don't know why
    I keep wishing this way."
Come along, black cat,
we have work to do.

LAMENT   *4/79*

I lament.
My heart is sad.
I'm in mourning.
I mourn my hope for love.

Is it dead,
    but seemingly would spring anew?
Shall I not cry inside?
I melt into the earth.
I weep my deepest tears.
I love you so,
(loved you)
    dreams and hopes for a loving life,
    dying,
    dead.
I would breathe life in your cold nostrils,
    though my faith we will survive,
    is nil.
I mourn.
I die.
I lament.

WHO SHALL BE THE WISER?   *4/79*

I must inhale
    the thick perfumes
    of the wild, love flower.
Come with me, lusty one,
    be my pregnant queen.
Let us meld,
    creamy, into the day
    and permeate the soil.

The third eye kept smiling.
I listened to the wind.
The day was ripped with sunshine.

I tasted chocolate peanuts.
Ed was sure I was right.

I see a vortex in the sky,
    the baby a lonely dot,
    sucked away by the wind.

The dull-eyed stare
    of the contented cow
    is not the breaking wave.

I'll not have my neck broke, twice.
Tearfully, in tones precise,
    across the blackened meadow,
    she called to me,
"I'll never come again."

Once hot oatmeal
    stifled the call of the loon
    across the Canadian lake.
But oranges hang high
    on dead-wood trees
    and blue jays appear
in the strangest places.

Lie with me, naked lady,
in full sun.
Who shall be the wiser?

FACE OF GOD

Why are you trapped behind those bars, my friend?
   I trapped myself.
A novel idea. But, to what gain?
   This way, I do not have to see the face of God.
I see. And is that so bad, the face of God?
   I don't know, I have never seen him.
Look, then!
   Are you God!?
No.
   I don't know where to look.
Why don't you want to see the face of God?
   I am afraid He will demand something of me.
And if he does?
   I shall not be able to give it.
Why not?
   He wants my only heart.
And can you not open it to him?
   No.
Why not?
   I have closed it forever.
Why so?
   If I open it, I shall see the face of Death.
And is that so bad, the face of Death?
   Yes.
Then you are afraid to see the face of God,
because he may require you to open your heart,
and if you do, you shall see the face of Death!
   Yes.
You stand here, then, afraid of God and Death.
   Yes.
A limbo state.
   Yes.
Afraid of God and Death.
   Yes.

ON COMPROMISE *5/79*

I hope to have exactly what I want
    with no compromise,
until disillusioned and too late,
    I find it impossible.
Then shall I compromise,
    but only a little.

MORE ANGUISH *5/79*

I have anguish
    in my heart.
Someone I cared for,
    (care for)
    is with me
    no more.
I miss her touch,
    her eyes, her kiss.
I miss her loving attention,
    her delicate beauty,
    the sweetness of her taste.
I wish she were with me.
And now, and yet,
    the ugly reservation
    rudely appears
    destroying the dream,
    her dream, my dream,
    exploding the love

   in my heart.
I have anguish.

I FEEL THE SOLID EARTH   *6/79*

I feel the solid earth
    like ... before me.
I bask in the healing ...
    of the midday sun.
I languish in the ...
    of the fragrant night
and listen with ...
    to the ... of life.
    I want to ...
and linger in the ...
    To live as if to ...
and love until I ...
    For this is where I ...
and want ...
    and do have.

I FEEL THE SOLID EARTH (Completed)   *6/79*

I feel the solid earth
    like a family of elephants before me.

and bask in the healing optimism
    of the midday sun.
I languish in the muted garden
    of fragrant night
and listen with all the focus of my being
    to the energies of life.
I want to revel in my living
    and linger in the arms of a mate,
to live as if to *catch-the-fox*
    and love until I pass beyond.
For this is where I take place,
    and I want my turn
as living creatures do,
    and I do have.

THE SPOTTED SNAKE   6/79

On the garden path,
    coiled, the spotted snake
    peacefully glistened.
She whispered love
    in honeyed tones
    to the gentle mouse,
    whose eyes, black with wonder,
    listened.
The yellow, spotted snake,
    whose sultry skin,
    harmoniously mixed
    with shades of brown and gray,
    spoke of love
    and life together,

    her reasons tight,
    like bricks in a wall.
The mouse, intrigued,
    could not deny the logic
    of this would-be mate,
    nor a quiet sense of death.

MIDNIGHT THOUGHTS 7/79

And now again
the earth is without form
and void and blackness
is upon the face of the deep.
Tired, vulnerable,
I sit on the edge of tears,
afraid of night's blackness.
An internal grieving
sucks me away.
I would that I'd blow away
the way the wind blows,
as a leaf,
swiftly over the hill,
and the wind in it's whistling,
as it whips the sky,
leaves white streaks.
I see the mountains
rise against the sun.
Immense, our planet,
great in it's turning.
Pinpoints of light
penetrate the blackness,

itchy like prickles,
sour like pickles.
A lion roars,
and on the continent,
terror fills the heart
of fleshy, animate food.

*Nonsense is
as nonsense does.*

I like potatoes
when they're mashed up tight.
Sing me a song before I sleep,

*"I love peaches in the mourning,
    but sometimes the night,
and a little pot of tea,
    infiltrates my room,
and a piece of toast will do,
    penetrates my flesh,
to begin a sunny day,
    assuring my doom."*

My heartbeat will drive it out!
Replace the cold terror
with warm flesh,
content in the afternoon.
And the evening sleeps,
having been sung to
by frogs and crickets
and creeping things.

I do love daisies
blowing in the wind.

*"Listen to me, mamma,
hear how I cry,*

sing me a song, too,
so I won't die."

I have a little yellow wagon
that follows me around,
in which I keep my things.
Hello, loved one.
Have you had me to eat?
I hunger for you as well.
Please eat me with kissable lips.
Ply me with love 'til I bloom.
I'll speak quietly from my heart.
You'll listen quietly with your heart.
We shall speak,
heart to heart,
essence to essence,
soul to soul.
Not head to head,
nor eye to eye,
but breast to breast.
Our souls will speak
as we stand by
and have nothing to say.
Breast to breast,
heart to heart,
soul to soul,
we speak,
we know,
we love.
"I'm getting married in the morning."
The essence of life
is living.
The essence of sense
is sensing.
The essence of happiness
is being.

"Ding dong, the bells are going to chime."
I want a big round watermelon,
and I want to spit the seeds.
See the grass grow.
See the tree wave.
See the bush flow
in the heat, rising.
I see trees
shaking their heads at me.
I see roots
reaching into soil.
Sing to me some sweet song,
you with love to spare,
that I may sleep,
and sleeping,
come together.
It is time you and I
became good friends,
walked in the garden
of friendly love,
spoke as brothers speak,
strong, willful, loving,
stout of limb,
stout of heart,
stout of intent.
Listen to the <u>little</u> voices.
Sometimes I'd have an amplifier
that I could hear them better.
The essence of drawing
is to get it right.
To say what is meant.
To do what must be done,
as the plant does what must be done
to produce it's flower.
The essence of growth
is growing.
The essence of song is singing.

The essence of heart
is it's beating.
The essence of process,
is proceeding.
"Roll out the barrel ..."
A wine is rich
if aged in wood
and drunk in the right frame of mind.
And so is milk.
And I am a brick,
strong, static,
compressive, tight.
I sit on the ground
and like it here.
I am a stick,
flexible, light.
I bend when I want
and will not break.
I am a flag.
I fly on a pole.
And when I am flying,
I'm living.
Give me a penny
and I'll give you a dime.
For such is my gladness
and rich is my heart.
Give me your bike
and I'll give you my home,
for so do I like you,
rich as you are.
Give me your smile
and I'll give you my heart,
for ready it is,
enthusiastic, strong.
I love you,
tree, waving.
Blow me a kiss.

I love you, tall grass,
warm in the field.
I love you strong rain
striking my mouth.
I love you weariness.
Time for your sleep.
Contented, you sleep.
Goodnight.

A LOVE POEM *11/79*

I should have moved
    into her space.
I should have encroached, sweetly,
    into the place of her cheek and mouth.

I should have felt her hair
    against my cheek.
    and breathed her being.

I should have lightly
    grazed her chin
    with my lips,
    eyes, half closed.

I should have seen her lashes
    drop quickly down,
    and looked into her eyes,
    deeply,
    and smoothed her hair
    from her cheek,
    shadows darkening.

I should have told her,
   wordless,
     with my presence.

I FEEL THE LONG SILENCE   *12/79*

I feel the long silence,
and revel in the breezes of another time.
Descend on me, wintry stars,
bathe my heart in lemon sticks.
Cover me with shafts
of purest ice.
I love you, night,
and you,
cold winds whistling o'er my skin.
Listen to the silence
of resignment
and becoming.
Breathe the quiet air
of crystal night.
Linger in the shadows
of lost love.

WINTER RAINS *2/80*

I love winter rains
as I do cold winds
that whisper
in the hollows of my bones.
They sing,
those slippery hollows,
of immortal life
as well as death.
I love wintry fog
that settles, restless,
on the night
and then advances,
stiff and formal,
through my face.

I love brittle stars,
those of Orion's belt,
Venus and Mars.
They float on mist,
and winter rains run,
coolly,
in the hollows of my face.

And I love
stars and fog,
cold winds and rain,
and death,
as well as life.

THE LITTLE SHIP

I move forth,
bravely,
as a little ship,
from that place
like the sun
of warmth and strength,
afloat on the might of the sea,
to confront a future,
to fair well,
or flounder.
Insignificant am I
beneath the power
of the sun's rays,
among the forces
of the existing world,
against the restlessness,
the brilliance of the sky.
Powerful, impartial,
yet do I move.
Even in my anxiety
and hope,
and fear,
nevertheless,
I move forward
with all the fitness
and strength
and toughness
I have, that I can gather,
that resides in me,
do I move.

FROM THE TEEMING CENTER
OF THE AGITATED MIND *2/80*

From the teeming center of the agitated mind,
    she grew with a boundless power and a mindless speed.

Spilling life's blood into the turmoil of oblivion,
    crying from the inside of a soul turned black,
    she screamed her presence to the impartial night.

The hungry jackal's lowered their yellow eyes
    and resumed duties to their prey.

I prefer the sunny optimism of an ignorant daisy
    to the silent terrors of an ingrown mind, don't you?

Check which you prefer:

    ___the sated stillness of an emancipated cow,
            or
    ___the poverty of hollow bones on broken rocks?

She greeted me with full stomach pressing against her lungs,
    and said she'd overheard the stifled crying
    of the baby in the loft,
    as the sawdust sifted, softly,
    in the stillness of the gloom.

When I looked up, I saw black cats with yellow eyes
    leap through brittle-starred, black heavens,
    teeth bared, in an anticipatory grin,
    which made me quizzical.

I don't know why miniscule insects climb lofty anise plants,
    but then, neither does the shrimp boat
        gliding above it's shadow.

I feel sure another yesterday will be on us by tomorrow,
    and when yesterday is now,
        can tomorrow be far behind?

I feel sure that it can't be, don't you?

HE LEAPS   *3/80*

On the breakfast table
the young, fat cat,
eyes on the counter,
concentrates on his leap.

He leaps.

Paws outstretched,
eyes intent,
body tense.
He misses!
Tangled on the floor.
How surprising.
How discouraging.
How humiliating.
Especially, for a cat.
Until I remember;

He did leap.

THE VOICE IN THE MIST **3/80**

I don't know how long she had
been whispering to me in the dark,
but the clocks yellow hand
pointed suddenly to seven
and struck three times.

I turned again
for the fifth time
and settled into my dream.

White mist moves, cold,
along solemn shores
of a soft wave sea.
"When will you be back?"
(I resume my conversation.)
And the lonely voice,
lost in the mist

that lingers in hollows
of the soft wave sea,
replied to me,
"When the clock strikes seven."

"But, the hand points to three!"
(Anxiously, I cry!)

"What is your problem?"

The phrase drifts in the air,
then blends with the mist.

"But, I don't understand."
*(I lay on my back
on the cold, wet sand.)*

"You will," said the voice,
*"when the red moon lifts
from the tense, black sea,
you'll come to me."*

Perspiring, I wake.
The clock's yellow hand points to seven
    and strikes seven.

I pull back blankets
    and worry myself to work.

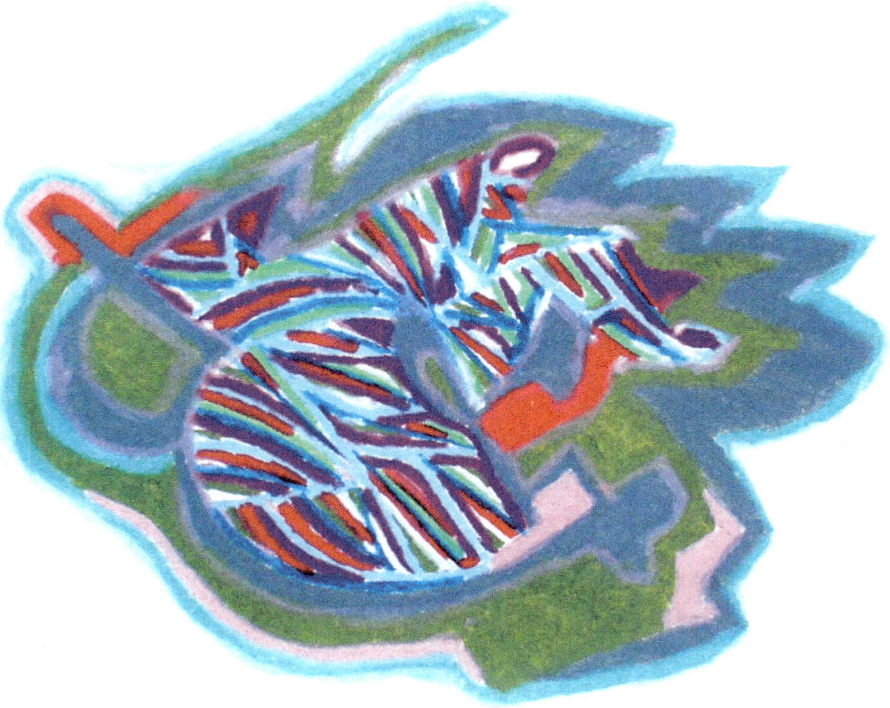

Fifteen

YOUR NATURAL RIGHT *3/80*

*B*eneath the black sea
of the abysmal mind,
lurking in the stagnant soup
of *"can't"* and being victim,
occupying space within
the thickness of, *"if only,"*
lives a dragon pure as sky.
Dragon, feel your strength!
Inhale the terrifying
richness of your soul.
Let loose that roar of devastation,
and let us see your leaping flame,
and feel your power of destruction.

Claim your space,
like the conquering sun,
and show the death and darkness
whom it is they fear.
Blister your inertia.
Fry your way to truth.
Burn your way to freshness,
and to freedom,
and to light,
your natural right.

THE CROW 3/80

The crow on the fence post
    sits, convinced.
He flaps and stretches,
    and assumes a pose
    of tense repose.
The sun is hot.
The crow, more so,
    because he is black.
His yellow eyes
    burrow deep
    into all he sees.
His expression, mean,
    behind his beak,
    unrelenting.
I wonder when he'll fly away.
He stays, it seems,
    for hours,
    watching, waiting,

    cocking his head,
    burrowing his mean eyes,
    staring, searching,
    observing.
Nothing escapes him.
What he doesn't see
    with his eyes,
    he feels through the quills
    of his feathers.
His essence is everywhere.
He permeates
    the atmosphere.
He stands, the center
    of his own aura
    of sensitivity
    and meanness,
    and I, the object,
    must *"cotton up"*
    or receive the big,
    "Or else!"
He sees in me
    something vile
    I see not within myself.
He does not see
     how beautiful I am.

SHALL I SEND YOU PLYWOOD   3/80

Shall I send you plywood
in the exact size
to nail over the hole
of your last escape?

Once self-nailed,
we could write graffiti
to tell of the act.

"Memorial to the triumph of defeat."
"They chose to cry in their beer."

They would not taste the food,
since it might have been too bitter
or too sweet.

"Here lies avoidance of life.
They were hopelessly afraid."

Were they to look us
anxiously in our eyes and shout,
    "We are afraid!"
    "We are afraid!"
then there would be hope.

And tears would come down,
and the plywood come down,
and the walls come down,
and the two would begin to walk.

Free!

ADORED   3/80

The rest of my life
is a blessing.

(Not in disguise.)
I listened to swallows
high on the wire.
They told me of love.
(I didn't know.)
To live in a group, adored,
that is the thing.
 "See here! You rascal!"

CONTENT, FREE, FALLING 3/80

I visualize myself
plunged into the darkness
of obliviousness and rain.
The wind howls from the north.
Living things are silent.
Streams of crystal water
peel away from pointed ends
of twigs and leaves
prostrate behind the gale.
There is no opening
in the black clouds.
Sleet from the fury
of the chaotic winds
stings my face and hands.
Yet I proceed
with joyous heart,
warm in my clothes
and free.
Let the wind howl and whine.
Let the rain bluster its way
through the long night.

I don't give a damn!
I'm free!
I'll follow my heart,
my trail,
my purpose or bent,
my whim or joy,
and the devil be damned!
I'll walk to the edge of the land
where the wind trails off,
and the rain streams over,
and the black night sky
opens below, as well as above,
and button my jacket
and leap.
I'll fall and falling, fall,
feel safe.
Secure in the warmth
of my body and spirit.
I'll fall through perpetual darkness
at home in a contented heart.
Falling, free, falling
through the night rain,
the sleet, the wind, the space.
That yawning, black, open space,
that immense womb
of the eternal living.
Contentedly, I fall, sure,
warm in my clothes.
Though storms howl about me,
and sleet stings my face.
Yet, I am smiling,
certain and content
in the warmth of my body heat
and invincible heart.
At peace in my clothes.
Falling through sleet,
and blackness,
and rain.

THE NON-LEAPING CAT *3/80*

The tombstone said
   "Here lies a cat
   who didn't leap."
The story goes,
He leapt once,
   and was severely punished.
He leapt twice,
   and was beaten for the trouble.
He leapt thrice,
   and was struck permanently down.
And he learned,
   as a smart cat should,
   that natural instincts,
   and leaping
   lead to punishment.
So he decided instead
   to walk,
   to sit,
   to lie down.
He'd sit on the table
   while other cats leapt,
   but would not leap.
Though, now and then,
   a glow in his eyes
   would give him away,
   a deep longing
   to fly through the air.
Nevertheless,
   his muscles turned to fat,
   and lost their elasticity,
   and he thought himself in circles,
   and read his eyes weary.
Other cats asked him,

"Why don't you leap?"
He would excuse himself
    for not leaping,
    for now he was too heavy.
After such a long time,
    there was deep confusion
    as to whether he *could* leap,
    for somehow,
    leaping and pain were the same.
His countenance evoked pity,
    and because another cat
    understood his plight,
(for something similar had befallen her)
    she took good care of him.
    Fed him.
    Petted him.
    Bedded him.
But even so,
    he did not live well.
And she did not live well.
    For how can one play
    with a non-leaping cat?

Eventually,
    the caring cat,
    with unmistakable leaping impulses,
    became annoyed.
(Was she missing something?)
And ...
    How does the story end?
Well, you read the tombstone.
    "Here lies a cat
    who wouldn't leap."
So he must have died.
    Unless I have the wrong story.
    (Maybe he lived to leap.)
And what happened

      to the pitying cat?
        Did she learn to leap?
I don't see her tombstone yet.

LOVE   *3/80*

Now the angels
from the darkened room
begin their incantations.
Like an expanding plant,
with startling speed,
fills the room,
so the hand of mind extends
to clasp a welcome soul,
and peace descends,
a golden joy,
like honey on an almond bun,
as love,
that solid heart,
lifts her hem,
and takes the throne.

BECOMING WHOLE *3/80*

Now that the intrepid adventurer
has dimmed the light
of youthful ardor
and has begun his advancing
in crazy swirls,
limp like a hand,
solid like a fist,
and the moons of Orion
are spilling their silvery light,
slow motion, into the emptiness,
to bathe the eyes of wonder,
stimulate the mind,
and wake the dormant heart,
I feel those gentle hands,
with billowing sleeves,
lifting my feelings
of reality,
and peace,
and love,
into the strong light
of truth,
as I become whole.

SONG OF THE PASSERBY *3/80*

The silver streaks
   of graying hair

fell gently to her shoulder,
    and on the steps
    of City Hall,
    the wind was getting colder.

The wintry winds, descending,
    blew cobwebs from her mind,
    and *"wisdom"* took it's rightful place,
    but not the proper kind.

Chorus:
So, I say,
"Bullshit, bullshit!
Won't you be my bullshit friend?
Bullshit, bullshit!
Bullshit - shit on you!
So, I say,
"Bullshit, bullsh...."
(Trails off in distance.)

MAGIC STONE   *3/80*

I have a magic stone
    through which I see
    the order of my life.
It is beautiful and rare
    like a moonstone,
    opalescent,
    textured,
    and just the proper weight.

It has organic
    surface patterns,
    designs,
    and arrangements,
    both irregular and smooth.
It is the stone
    that magnifies
    my life.
When I look intensely
    into it,
    the translucent stone
    becomes crystal clear,
    like deep water.
It magnifies anything
    at which I choose
    to look.
It brings whatever I desire
    into crystal clarity,
    optically correct,
    and pure.
Pock-marked, pitted,
    when first seeing,
    my stone,
    yet, when I look intensely into it,
    I see all I wish to behold,
    magnified and clear.

SHOW TIME   3/80

At night time
I sit with my back

against a stone wall in the patio.
I hold a tall poplar branch
high in the air,
extending above the wall.
A real poplar branch
from a strong, live tree
within the patio,
waves, blows, comes and goes.
I wave my branch, too,
in harmony with the living branch,
so that others,
when they see the branches waving
from beyond the wall,
will think my branch
springs from a living tree,
coming and going,
waving and blowing.
I cannot perfectly
imitate the real tree,
but I do put on
a reasonable show.

THUS, IT WILL EVER BE *4/80*

*M*y memory returns,
    jogged off center
    by strong winds
    blistering
    between canyon walls,
    clean and crisp.

Razor edges of black shadows
    cut the mind
    in tan and black,
leaving the, *"three's a pageant,"*
    Mars, Jupiter, Venus
    in their precisely
    changing patterns,
    to freeze in the blackness
    of outer space,
    shimmering their messages
    to waiting eyes
    and waiting minds,
    calling to the souls of man,
    the species.

From the inception
    they've danced the answer,
    yet, we do not perceive it,
    not having the proper sensors,
    but only minds
    and beautiful bodies.

We sit,
    ignorant bumpkins,
    and dangle our legs
    over the black chasm,
    and ask our silly questions,
    and the celestial pageant answers,
    and we do not understand,
    and so, we ask again,
    and the answer's
    in the very air.

Yet, we hear or see it not,
    but continue to ask,
    and so on,
    and so on,

generation upon generation,
and I suspect,
thus,
it well ever be.

NOTES FROM THE UNCONSCIOUS   *4/80*

Why not
 the intrepid daisy?
For who can taste
 it's journey to the dying sky?
I'd like to
 whistle up some pig meat
 myself, little darling,
 at least enough
 to last us 'til we're home,
 content, in bed.
The zoo is the place for you,
 silly one.
Can't you make your silly way
 through this vast garden?
Here, don't you like this
 yellow rose,
 or this bright daffodil?
Reminds you of yourself,
 does it?
Well! No wonder,
 the way you've been eating
 these soggy days.
It's a wonder
 you've not got

    jock-rot of the cerebellum.
Well, give it time,
    give it time.
You'll know what to do
    when you're
    just a little older.
Of course, the great horse trader
    in the sky
    may be after you by then
    with his divine lasso.
But who is the wiser?
    I don't whistle Dixie
    to everyone,
    especially
    when I'm sober.

GOOD "OLD" DAYS   *4/80*

*H*ey, there,
simple minded soul!
What have you got to chew on?
Do you like your life?
Or is it a pain
in the you-know-what?
Maybe the golden goose
will give you his egg.
But then,
might as well
hope to walk on water.
I know a magic jackass,

but he's too stubborn to move.
I'm tired of waiting.
Maybe the stars
will become confused,
forget which way to turn,
zag then zig,
this way, that way,
in swooping patterns
bumping into each other
in some mad night display.
Will that answer
your crazy question?
Or the clouds may become
a solid chunk,
and fall, plunk,
on the ground.
Or the rocks
float away
like the red balloon
from the picture
of the same name.
Or the sun,
flare bright blue
and go out,
leaving it's after image,
dissolving,
slowly
on your retina.
I know little tricks
with which to trick
the mind.
Tricky Dick,
they'd call me,
in them days
of common nonsense.
Them days when we'd
read the funny papers

with *"Happy Jack."*
Those were the days
when stars were stars,
and in their proper place.
Those were the days
when clouds were clouds,
and a rock was a rock
and the sun stayed up
all day 'til night
and, *"Time to go to bed,
there's school tomorrow!"*
"<u>Good</u>" old days,
not like these,
good *"<u>old</u>"* days.

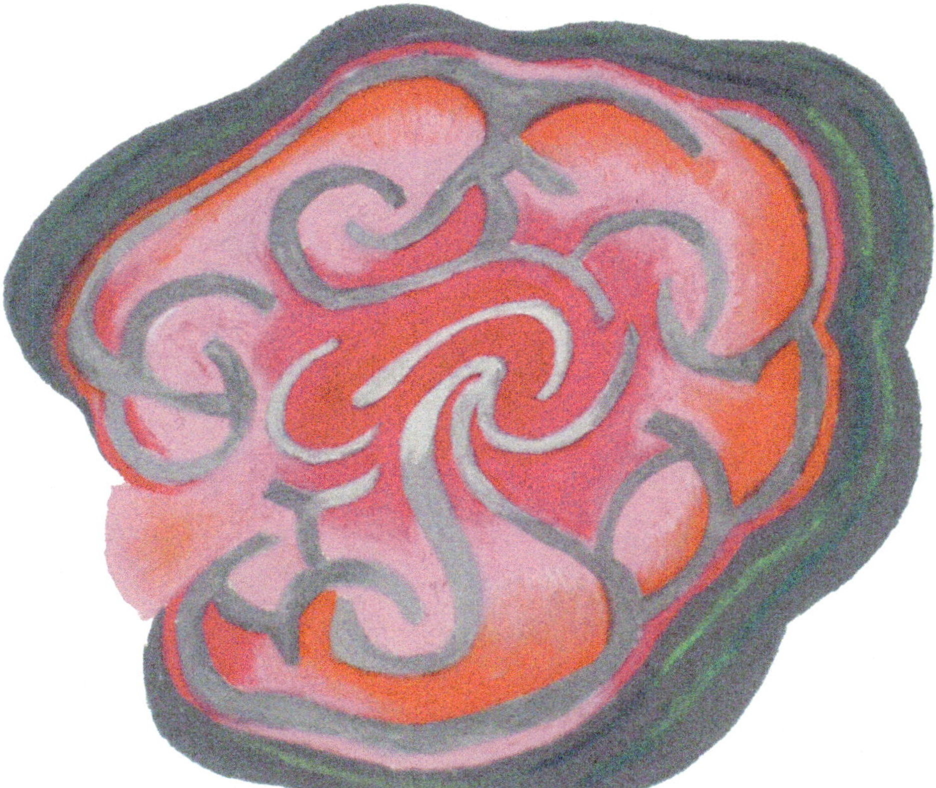

Sixteen

RELATIONS OF SIX *4/80*
(Short humorous story)

    *P*urity was Sally
        Sweetness, chaste,
with a white dress,
    primly,
        and light,
tied at the waist,
    with a pretty red
        belt
and a bow in her
    shiny brown
        clean

as a mountain air
   stream and as
      fresh
as a dew studded
   iris,
     untainted,
   and highly naive,
   romantically
     said
"How do you do?"

Maxmillian, old sage,
   gnarled as a trunk,
encrusted with swarthily
   bony-skin, hairy,
and hairs on the backs
   of his knobbly-veined hands,
and warts in a clump at the side
   of his roving-eye nose,
sat in the black shadows,
   cast, as a rotating eye
riveted hers in a gravelly,
   gruffy, *"What do you want?"*
And S. Sweetness
   sweetly replied,
"I want a prince."

Ruford Rake,
   that gallant snake.
Dapper hat, straight
   on an off-center head,
smiled a charlatan,
   white-toothed smile.
Some real talent,
   with patches of flake,
dressed in snappy clothes,
   white tie, suit.

Slippery sweet talk
   leapt to his tongue,
and he bowed with a,
   "How about me?"

Penny Practical
   calls a spade a spade,
a somewhat cynical
   rusty spade.
She's been through
   the wheat mill.
Knows what's what.
   Can tell you
a thing or two.
   In tacit touch
with the here
   and now,
a thought for a
   thought,
as well as an
   eye,
countered with
   jealousy,
bitter,
   "Ee's not for you!"

Ruford Rake,
   "See here!
     I do!"

Paula Paranoid,
   mother-frumpy,
worries incessantly
   all about trivia.
Essence of forehead
   and wrinkly
brow, the hard-working

face,
fatted up to the fence
   and tootled a
singy-song,
   "Sally! Oh, sweetness, pure!
   Time to come home
   to the home of your
   homey, sweet home!"
and dropped her
   hand
from her rather large mouth
   to her pneumatically,
polka-dot hip.

Bruce Bumpkin,
   county bumpkin,
thick as a
   rope,
full as a fatted,
   handsome calf,
with L'il open
   Abner eyes,
surprised
   and wondered,
amazed at
   everything,
   awestruck
   just to be alive.
That growing tree.
That shining cloud,
   could only inquire,
"Ah! What did you say?"

Paula Paranoid,
   "Not talkin' to you!"

"There's your prince!"
    said practical Penny
to Sally Sweetness,
    and to her, she said,
"Ask Maxmillian,
    the ugly old sage."
Miss Sweetness
    queried,
"Uncle Max?
Shall I truly
marry Bruce?"

Uncle Maxmillian
    snorted and snuffled,
chortled and chunneled,
    and sputtered an ancient,
old gruff, *"Please do!*
Yes! My dear, marry Bruce!"
And to the bumpkin
    he next conferred
in learned tones,
"Come to the light
at the top of your head
and twist the switch
to Sally Sweetness,
your heart's desire,
and live under cover
of wondrous,
if not, bliss."

The two joined hands
    in an open-eyed stare.
Each to the other,
    we leave them there.

And Ruford Rake,
    sidling up

to Practical Penny,
    both join hands.

Paula Paranoid,
    pumped in her pride,
and placed her pink
    little pinky inside
the hoary old hand
    of Uncle Maxmillian
and frumpily giggled
    a missing tooth,
        "I'll take you!"

But sage Maxmillian
    harrumphed his humph
and grumbled a minimum,
"Ah! Thanks a lot,
but this slow China Boat,
you see, is leaving tonight
and,
regrettably,
I'll be sailing away
to the Hong side
of Kong,
but I do wish you luck."

IF SHE COULD COPE   **4/80**

*H*er face was taught,
her lips pursed,
restrained, not talking.

Her forehead, tight,
vertical lines between her eyes.
She speaks not,
but only looks.
God knows what she sees.
God knows what gross thoughts
lie inside that solid bone.
Veins in her neck,
a tree-trunk system
to carry her head,
hair unkempt and blown.
Would she but shriek!
Would she but cry out!
Would she but cry.
Would she but try.
Then I could hope.
Then she might learn to cope,
and I could rest.

HAPPY BIRTHDAY   *4/80*

*H*appy birthday, foot!
Walked on any water lately?

Happy birthday, arm!
Waved any good-byes, today?
Any hello's?

Happy birthday, brains!
Had any good thoughts
with which to occupy yourself?

This is the 19,176th
day of our life.
What a glorious day
to be alive, folks!
One of the best I've ever had.
I still see pretty well,
and hear pretty well,
and the rest of my senses
haven't suffered much
for being almost
20,000 days old.

Happy birthday, self!
You've done a good job
just living this long.

I sure am proud of you,
and wish you
19,000 more
beautiful days of life,
even better
than the last 19,000.
Happy birthday, me!

SANTANA WIND 4/80

The Santana wind
is at it again.
Whistling down
old Carbon Canyon,
flushing my room

with dry,
    cool,
       air.
Roaring through
the Eucalyptus leaves,
eager to get to sea.
Time to stay up tonight.
North wind time
is not for sleeping,
but for staying up
and writing thoughts
and thinking about
what's done,
what's doing,
what's going to be done.
Old Santana wind
is whipping it up,
cutting the face of the rocky cliffs,
trampling the tall spring grass,
forcing living things into their spaces
and flushing them out
    with cool,
       dry,
Santana air,
washing my living space too.
Flushing thoughts.

THE JUMPER   *4/80*

The man in the red suit
    leaps
from the high plane,
    opens
his artificial red wings
    and plummets,
      head down,
in tight circles,
    toward earth.

At the critical moment,
    falls back,
releasing his wings
    that float back,
      up, off
and out of sight.

With precise
    gymnastic form,
executes
    a perfect,
      mid-air
front jump.

The man
    in the red suit,
falling free,
    feet first,
      toes pointed,
      knees of steel,
      hands to sides,
      spine erect,
      shoulders down,

head and neck aligned,
confident,
    at 2,000 feet,
hurtling,
    feet first,
toward the bay
    and cold water.

He approaches the water,
    and with perfect timing,
jack-knifes,
    head first,
    into the cold bay.
He does not sink,
    but pops up fast.

Later, in the outboard,
    we pick him up.

A tanned oriental face,
    strong jaw,
    clear eyes,
    intelligent.
His head and torso
    like an ancient ivory sculpture.
His shoulders thick and wide,
    his chest slim and strong.
I think I detect
    a long scar
at the side of his ribs,
    then, startled,
I see
    his upper arms
    are merged with
    and have grown
    to the sides of his chest.

We return through the lobby,
    the jumper, shirtless,
in tie-up pants
    and thongs.
I find, recently,
    it is of general knowledge
he is a champion boxer
    as well.

JOY OF MUSIC   4/80

Music from another place,
another time,
thrills my senses.
Why should music
make my heart
feel so joyfully,
wonderfully alive?

I'm receiving
the essence, the spirit,
the core and nature
of love.

The tones and time,
the melody and rhyme,
are the instrument
through which a musician,
    from another time,
    another place,
sends his or her love,

and it is love's affection,
    or expression,
that thrills my senses,
    makes my heart
    feel wonderfully alive,
and I, listening
    and receiving love,
am joyful.

MARSH BIRDS   4/80

On the damp ground
by the lake in the meadow,
    still,
    among the bull-rushes,
I heard the marsh birds
    sing a dimensional song.
Six, or so, where in the band.
One exactly in the bush.
One to the right at fifty paces.
One in the tree
    at the edge of the pond,
and others
    precisely in their places,
high and low,
    in various directions and distances,
    calling,
    answering
    chortling,
    discussing,
glorified me in their mystic conversation.

And I, the magnificent center,
with eyes and ears and brain,
enjoyed the primordial gentleness,
the archetypal sweetness,
the ancient eloquence
of this most unique,
dimensional song.
It seemed performed just for me
by a little known group called
    the Marsh Birds.

THE ABANDONED TRUCK   *4/80*

The abandoned truck,
    inert,
digs its green snout
    into the loose foliage.
Its raised hood
    opens
toward the windshield,
where a phantom driver
    might see
the disintegrating engine,
    and the spider's webbing
    across the fan-belt.
Irregular splotches
    of rust emerge
from heavily oxidized paint,
and the trucks sideboards
    are wracked and decayed.

The steering wheel,
        disengaged,
lies on cover-less seat springs
        seen through the door,
where the driver's window
        has dropped to its final resting place.
The truck paralyzed as in a dream,
        and helpless.
Within the rude metallic forms,
tall mustard weeds
        establish their intimacy
and tiny yellow flowers
spring from beneath the flat,
bald, rubber tires,
        now separated from their rims.
This strange vision,
this culmination
of logical thinking,
this ruined symbol
        of man's eternal aspiration,
lies at the halfway point
        between usefulness
        and delight,
and its return to dust
and Mother Earth.

I wonder
if we can get
this sucker
started?

BOY IN BLUE JEANS

The boy in the blue-jeans
        carrying the yellow pail
walked across the lot
        blowing a whistle.
Seen from the back,
        the boy in the blue T-shirt,
left elbow straight,
        grasping the wire handle,
the pail, empty,
right elbow bent,
        right hand to his mouth,
holding the whistle and blowing,
        walked across the parking lot.
The boy in the blue-jeans and T-shirt,
        whistling and walking,
swinging the empty yellow pail,
blowing his athletic whistle
        in short blasts,
pursued his work
        to fill the bucket,
        clean the walls,
        wash the floors,
the pail of soiled water,
having been emptied on parking lot plants.
A boy in blue T-shirt and jeans
        crossed the parking lot,
        grasping the wire handle
        of the empty yellow pail,
left arm straight, right arm bent,
        holding the athletic whistle
to his lips, and blowing short blasts,
        holding the pail,
walked across the parking lot.

THE BLUE PENCIL SPINNING   *4/80*

*T*he blue pencil
    sleeps on my table
casting a pointed gray shadow.
I feel it thinking.
I feel it awakening.

Trembling with energy,
it lifts to the air,
    invisibly powered,
flies to the wall,
    and inscribes
the single word,
    Freedom!
The blue pencil
    glides
to the center of the room
and hovers, weightless,
before beginning
    a slow turning,
    a revolving,
    end over end,
    eraser over point,
with increasing speed,
until I detect a low
    hmmmm!

I see the blue-blur-disk
    spinning, humming,
    mid-air,
    before me.

The blue pencil-disk-blur,
    humming,

begins an acceleration,
    and as the revolutions
    per second increase,
the pitch of the humming
    becomes higher.
The blue-disk-whir
becomes less visible.
The pitch becomes a whine.
The whine becomes a whistle.
The visibility, ever less,
    and whistle so high,
I can no longer hear it.
    At the moment
I no longer hear it,
I no longer see it!

ONE LANE ROAD 4/80

The sign said,
"One lane road,"
intended to mean
only one lane passable,
that automobiles
using the same lane
in opposite directions
might collide
head-on, leading to
a real life nightmare
such as,
the sound of breaking glass,
the hallucinatory vision

of crushed metal,
and rolling hubcaps,
the deadly silence that hangs
like poison gas
on still night air.
Silence broken only by
whimpering and dripping sounds.
The interminable wait.
The sound of a siren winding down.
Rotating red and yellow lights.
The real.
The unreal.
The mixed sense
of timelessness and urgency.
The tire skid marks.
The odd positioning.
The people.
The sign sheared off at the base,
Lying in the ditch, face up.
The sign said
"One lane road"
Intended to mean
only one lane passable,
that automobiles
using the same lane
in opposite directions
might collide,
head-on,
leading to ...

THE WALKING CLOCK

I have a clock
    that takes one step
    every tick.
(We walked to Ventura, one day.)
Each tick takes one second.
Each step carries it forward
    three feet.
In one minute
my clock walks 180 feet.
In one hour
    it walks 2 miles.
It walked for 27 days,
    one time,
(I wound it well.)
and fell from the edge of the earth
    into space.
I followed it with my binoculars.
    Soon, it reached
    the velocity of light,
and during each tick,
    traveled 186,000 miles.
But at that speed,
    I could no longer hear it.
Sound, traveling at 1100 feet per second,
    could only recede from my ears
at the rate of 185,999 and 4/5ths
    miles per second.
Fortunately I have a good telescope, too,
    and could see the clock face clearly.
It fell into the sun's gravity field,
    not without a peek
at venus and mars,
then came looping back to earth.

(From outer space.)
My clock, still ticking,
roared through the atmosphere
at 9:51 and 20 seconds, P.M.
    Its outer shell,
being made of titanium,
    saved it from burning.
I found it Saturday morning
    on top of Mount Lassen
    (while picnicking)
    in a snow drift
    at 10:02 A.M.
What time it really was
while my clock was in outer space
    is pure speculation.
My clock yet ticks, merrily,
though it appears somewhat blackened
    and scorched
    by its ordeal in the heat and cold.
I've set the alarm to go off
    in the morning
at approximately 16 miles.
(7:00 A.M., Sunday.)
Luckily, it's on a miniature treadmill,
    calibrated at 3-feet per second,
and I've closed the bedroom doors
    and secured the screens
    just in case.

ONE SPIRIT 4/80

The crescent moon
came stealing across the country highway.
It's quiet light
permeated the cornfields and cornstalks,
and sifted it's chalky powder
deep into the wheat-fields
rising in the summer night.
The pavement shone
like thousands of moonstones
laid in a silvery ribbon
lacing the black hills.
Venus lifted her head
just above the mountainous ridge,
and other stars
assumed their places
in the blue-black heavens.
It was time for me
to meld myself
into my essence
and assume one spirit,
indivisible.

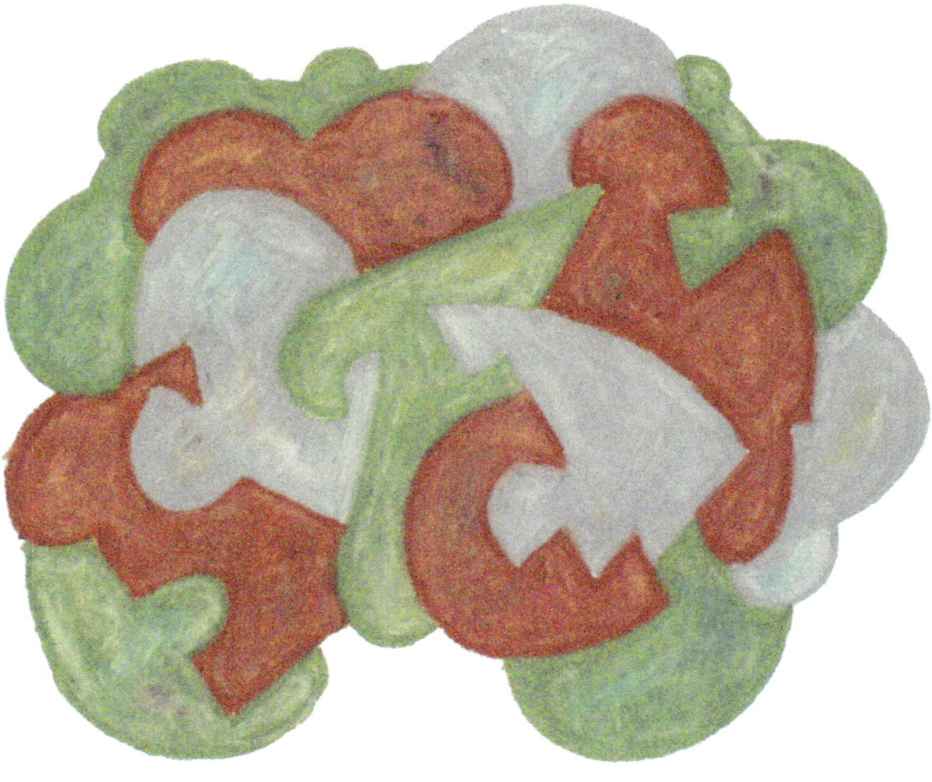

Seventeen

PITH OFF *4/80*

*W*hen eating an orange
Grandmother used to say
   she liked the pith.

(That's the soft, spongy tissue in the center of the orange.)

Webster says *"pith"*
   means *"the essential part, gist, or strength"*
   and *"full of meaning or force."*

A novel such as <u>War and Peace</u> is full of pith,
   or pithy.

When eating an orange this morning,
    I removed the skin with a knife,
    not too carefully, I suppose,
    and when I cut it into sections,
    there was considerable spongy tissue
    clinging to the segments.

When I ate them,
    the spongy tissue from under the skin
    tasted much like pith.
    (I ate the pith, too.
    It was delicious.)

I said to myself,
    "This is really a pithy orange,
    full of gist and strength,
    full of meaning and force.
    I feel healthier when I eat this pith."

Then a piece of pith fell on my shirt.
    I got pith on myself,
    but that was not the end of the world.

The next time you eat an orange,
    notice the white tissue
    beneath the orange skin
    tastes much like pith,
    and for God's sake, be careful.

Don't get pith on yourself.

THE WORDS ARRANGE THEMSELVES   *4/80*
(From a dream)

*U*pon awakening,
the following words
arrange themselves
as in a vision,
before me.

"*I sit,
a dynamite packet of seeds,
beneath a wavy line of the 'tizzies,"*

which I take to mean,
my potential self
is submerged beneath,
or subordinated to
my present self.

I find this
difficult to admit,
but dreams don't lie
and to dream
and find the words
arranging themselves,
as in a vision,
before me,

"*I sit
with my full potential extending
high above a wavy line of my former "tizzies,"*

is obviously, my present task.

PATH DIVIDING   5/80

Freshly arrived
from a darkened world,
defenses intact,
I walk a path
dividing maturity from death.

The death,
a life of *"acting out,"*
driven by a force within.

(Not my conscious self.)

Maturity,
    an act of living life,
    expansive,
    aware.

POWER STAR   5/80

As some mighty river
    pours from the cliff edge,
surges of power
    invest my soul.

Banks of snowy water falling,
    inch by inch,
in rhythmical sheets,

into the chasm where maelstroms,
   swirling pools,
   and eddies,
   suck and spew forth,
   until, lazily and deep,
meandering returns,
   and I am midstream,
   riding high and calm,
sun-charged and glowing.

Mountains, hanging cliffs and boulders,
   pock-marked with age, drift by,
while I lay dreaming.

I see thunderclouds
   mount the sky,
   as I drift, stealing
beneath the blue mantle,
and then, quietly,
Jupiter.

TWO, I KNOW   *5/80*

I know a fine potential
arrested in sameness,
frozen in attitude,
petrified, stuck.

I know a personality
trapped in a block,
or blind, *(in a trance)*
motionless, inert.

But also I know
a fluid disposition,
vital as ocean,
surging in depth.
A shifting variety,
or as a river,
gently flowing,
diversified, growing,
within transitions mutant way.

THE IMPOSSIBLE DREAM 5/80

I dreamed
the impossible dream
and sure enough,
it was impossible.

ON THE BRINK 5/80

*O*n the brink of great discovery,
    anxiously I sit.

(Something more than inspiration.)

Waiting for it's great descent,
    like for a giant purple bird,
    I wait
    for a flow to infuse my blood
that I may passionately move
    in the river's mighty center.

I wait for some knowledge
    to claim my mind,
    my body,
    my passion,
    my soul,
to lead me with purpose to a sweetened end.

Perhaps it's living through process,
    delightful in its moments,
    as in a sprout springing,
    or a tender morn singing.

(Only at death, do we know life.)

For some immense discovery,
    expectantly, I sit,
    tense and yearning,
    listening, alert,
    concentrated,
    burning.

A fluid process, forming,
will take me where I'll go,

to feed me intravenously.
so my energy will flow.

I HUM 'DE DUM, DUM 9/80

*I*n the park,
I hum 'de dum
and beat the drum
and hum 'de dum,
          dum.
It's very dark,
and I wiggle my bum
'til my ears are numb,
though dogs bark.
Let them come
and hum 'de dum,
while I beat my drum
in the dark, park,
and hum 'de dum,
          dum,
and bark.

GIVE ME SOME SKIN, PAL 9/80

*T*houghts, as on a screen,
in shades of gray and white,
fearsomely projected.

Sounds of running feet
    on dust,
      broken glass,
      and bottle caps.

Disintegrating buildings
    flashing past.
Dilapidated alleyways
    pouring
from the corners of my eyes.
    and all those lies,
    and all that fuzz
    without any peach,
    and all that living
    without any giving.
Put 'er there, pal,
    that's all in the past.
Give me some skin, pal.
    I see you at last.

Fade out, dark screen.
Fade in, new scene.

THROUGH THAT DOOR *10/80*

*T*hrough that door,
beyond which
lies the darkness
of the unconscious mind,

I plunge my fist

and reach through
the broken hole,
and close my hand,
grasping.

I know not what delight,
or horror
I shall find, wriggling,
as I withdraw.

NO EXPECTATIONS *10/80*

*H*aving fallen
   within the convoluted catacombs
of lost dreams and great expectations,
   I am now emerged,
and walk the fertile gardens
   of *HALLELULJA,*
with <u>no</u> expectations.

Hear me now,
   you within,
for you are made of solid stuff,
   those as dreams are made of,
strong as an arrow
   shot from a Souix-bow.
Collect your wits,
   my newfound friend,
and travel for a while
   with Kings and Princesses.

Let the dead remain buried
   in silver-laid coffins,
   and to the welcome sleep
   of peacefulness at last,
   and come, instead, with me

to the lofty mountains
of growth and understanding.

THE BIG LESSON *10/80*

*M*y frustration,
    hapless, hopeless, helpless,
camps on my doorstep.

Why must everlasting filth
romp through wellsprings of life?

How can the Godhead,
    in alliance with time and nature,
contribute to such antiquated demagoguery?

    Damn you, helplessness!

I hate you,
    and will rejoice you hanging by your heels.
Especially after my gifts of time,
    energy,
    money,
I find it hard now to <u>expect nothing.</u>

Apparently that's the big lesson,
    feeling lucky with a kick in the face.

FREE? *4/81*

For the first time,
the tornado came,
howling, rushing, tumbling into ...
Love, the golden petals
    of a simple native bush,
has me spinning!

I see the multi-layered sparkling
on the horizon an instant before ...

Takes to the wind, speeding,
    rocketing skyward,
    long tail streaming.

Feel the freshness of the air
    tingling on the skin.
The clouds, for once with purpose,
from the inner ... inside,
    beginning from the center,
    expanding, billowing,
rising against the richness ...
    rich blue, blueness
of the atmosphere beyond.

Ever richer, darker blueness ...
Until the brightness of a single star.
The pointedness, the brittleness
of a special star,
    ties all together,
becomes the catalyst, the essence, the object
to which there is only flowing toward.

And the star,
> and the clouds,
> and the object, myself,
rising against ...,
> long tail streaming free,
yet grounded
> by an imperceptible wire
tied to the ground – connected.
Free, yet tied back.

LONGING, SLEEPING, BEDDING, LOVING　　　*9/81*

I long to sleep
in the bed I love.

I long to love
in the bed I sleep.

I bed too long
in the love I sleep.

I long to bed
in the sleep I love.

I sleep too long
in the bed I love.

I bed too long
in the sleep I love.

I love too long
in the bed I sleep.

THE CROAKING CRICKET *9/81*

The croaking

cricket

cried to me.
I raised my hand.
I turned my head.

I would not hear

the croaking cricket's

choking tear.

Quietly.

Quickly.

The cricket

. . . .

croaked.

CONVERSATION

*H*i der, brudda! What you doin'?

    Goin' for a walk.

You goin' fo a walk?

    Ya! I goin' fo a walk.

Kin I go wit you?

    I don' care, I got nuttin' to do anaway.

Hey! This sho is fun, walkin wit you
   down dis dirt road.

    What?

I say ...

    Ne' mine.

OK! Hey! Ain' dis a graveyard we walkin' pass?

    I don' know.

Yeah! It is! Lookee dem big stones.
   Hyeah! Wait up! I gonna look!

    Pshaw!

Hey! Dis say,   "Here ly ol' uncle Jed.
                         Needed food 'n water.
                         Couldn' get outa bed."

    I say, Pshaw, agin!

Ain' much ov fa pome, is it?

    I think it's ratty!

Gravedigger: Hey! Where you guys goin'?

We jus' walkin' pass. Dis a shoat-cut
    to where we're goin'.

Gravedigger: Don' fall in no holes. Hyuk! Hyuk! Hyuk!

Ha! Ha! Das a good one, missa grave-digga,
    we won'. Gooa-bye!

    Boy! I shoo don' wan' be buried in no col'
    groun' Pshaw!

You don' lak it?

    Whoooee! Jus' too damp. Can't breathe
down der. Not fo' me!

What we gon' do wit you, den, afta you pass 'way?

    I gon' get creemated, das what.

You shoo you know what you talkin' bout?

    Shoo I do! You kin kreemate ma bones,
    den skatter de ashes in de ocean.

You lak water?

    Sho do.

Thas too col' for me.

> *Hey, man! You not goin' to feel it
> when you daid.*

Too wet! fish's might git ya.

> *I don' care.*

How you goin' skatter de ashes,
    fum a plane or sumptin'?

> *Sho nuff. Plane jus' fine.*

Wha' kine plane? Lak, say ... jus a light-blue,
    2-seater job?

> *Yeah! Gess so.*

Not a 747 or nuttin' like dat?

> *Naw! How you gon' open da windows
> ona 747. They don' work.*

I s'pose the steward's cud throw de ashes out de do'.

> *Oh, man! Git away fum me! Why don' you
> walk ova thea? I don' hav' ta take this!
> Throw th' ashes offa 747? Thas dumb!*

Don' git huffy with mee!

> *Well, you so stupid!*

I was jus' askin', thas all.

> *Well, ass' me sumtin' intelligent.*

How 'bout a 'heli-copter' Could we throw yur
   ashes out de do' of a 'heli-copter'?

> *Man, have you eva bin under a 'heli-copter'*
> *when it's goin'?*

No. Gess not.

> *The blades jus' blow th' ashes*
> *eva-which-a ways. They jus' fly*
> *all ova th' place.*

Yeah! Gess yur right.

> *When ahm ded, you kin cre-mate me*
> *an skatta ma ashes from a glider-plane.*
> *That would be jus' fine. No noise.*
> *Jus' peaceful – whooosh, whoosh*
> *of de air goin' by.*

That soun' n-i-i-i-i-ce.

> *Yeah! You kin do it that way.*

You wan' me ta skatter 'em slow-like,
   in a long line, or what?

> *Hell, man, I don' care!*

Well, I wan' to git it right. I cud trow 'em all at once
   in a big lump. I cud jus throw de bag
   ova-board – an das it! No foolin' 'roun.

> *You know what, man?*

Course, a pelikan mought catch 'em mid-air
   an' eat it. Den where you be?

You know what, man?

What?.

Ahm goin' this way now. See you later.

I go wit' you!

Ne' mine. I kin make it myself.

Well don' go 'way mad, brudda. I jus' tryin' t' help.

Don' need no help. Goodbye!

PSHAW!

COTTON MAN DREAM   2/82
(From a dream)

We moved to a new house in the field
and had put everything in order
when the earth-shift cracked the floor
and my brother fell into the wall.
I cried a frightened warning
and put out a threatening fire,
then ran from the house to a junk pile
and found a useable frame for a dune-buggy.
Returning, I met the dirt-faced man,
(the ghost of the house)
who shoved papers down my shirt.
I tried to understand the ghost

and searched his face for meaning,
until, feeling threatened,
I Karate-kicked him midsection
and the ghost folded, collapsed like a doll.
I said,
"There, I knew you were a cotton man!"

THROUGH THE NOSE 2/82

And I say unto you, friends,
be with us, for times are changing,
and the essence of our final stages
will be in the everlasting sun.
With eternal power,
it will plunge itself into our hearts
and you will know,
as I know,
that the only way to heaven
is through your nose.
This may strike you foolish,
yet think on it
and you will realize that it is you,
and only you *(if not me)*,
that can solve this dilemma,
and I am here, offering what I can,
and I urge you to use me,
for it is to your gain,
and also to mine,
if you see it that way.

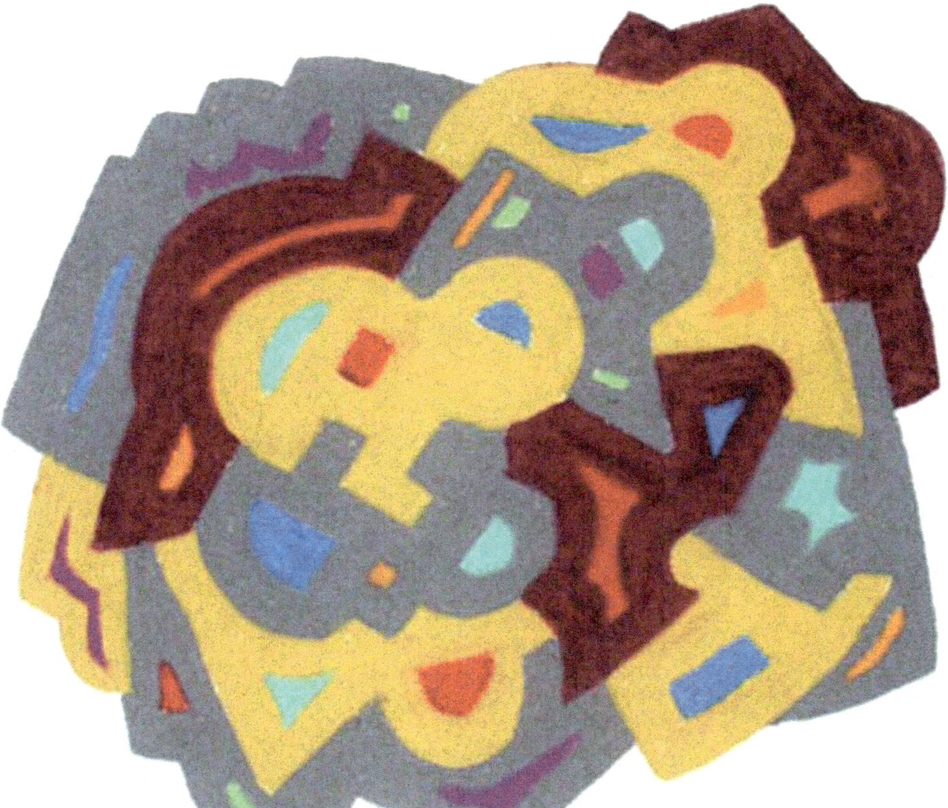

Eighteen

WHERE ARE YOU NOW? *2/82*

Where are you now,
cold winds that froze my soul?
Have you returned to Hell?
Will you plague me again?
I would you'd keep to yourself
and stew and grumble
among the likes of your own kind.
I would that I could breathe the fresh air,
worry-free and careless, once again,
but my knowledge of your
black and formless presence
has seeped into the roots of me,
and I know it as not a question,

*"Will you rise again, but
<u>when</u> will you rise again?"*
I shall learn to fight you on your own terms,
or I won't.

WHERE ARE YOU RAIN?   *2/82*

Where are you rain
to wash my thoughts?
I listen for your soothing patterns.
Caress me with soft droplets.
Free me, my self-bound ties.
Sweep me into freshened air.
Hold me, cool, in showery peace.

UNCOMFORTABLE AT NIGHT   *2/82*
(From a dream)

Uncomfortable in the night,
clearly form the words
from the darkness of my mind,
"I have no faith in you."
Image of a fragile room
close to waters edge.
At night the breakers strike

the flimsy painted plywood room
that I've designed
to house my sleeping child
who fitful cries,
"I have no faith in you."
What have I done?

IT DOESN'T SEEM QUITE REAL   *2/82*
(Enlargement - from a dream)

*I*t doesn't seem quite real!
A poorly constructed house
    cantilevering over water's edge.

Foreboding gray ocean
    in heavy seas, lying in wait beyond the mist.

White foam and hiss of run-up.
It seemed a child I knew once lived there.
I must enter the house.
Such a rickety old place.

The surge striking it, running along its sides,
    feeling its push, the pull of the back-wash
    tugging at creaking walls,
        coaxing it, inviting it into gray water.

I felt strange in there.

Just one room, really,
    with one small window, elbow high,

looking into gray bleakness.
I looked out the window.

I didn't like looking out the window.
The sea was grim and threatening.
What lurked beyond the mist?
Some giant wave, no doubt, to do me in.

This ancient, crippled building
    would break off and I'd be swept with it
    out to sea, where beyond the mist,
    it would sink,
    disappear, silently, into gray depths.
    I'd perish, alone.

The peak of high tide is happening.

That one mighty breaker of the highest tide,
    an immense wave, ran shoreward by the open door
    taking the cracked wooden steps with it,
    loosening the structure, irrevocably,
    from its foundations.

When it returns, it shall surely carry us out to sea.
If I jump out the door,
    I'll enter raging water and
    be carried into wild surf, alone.

Here comes the back surge.
The flimsy shed is jarred from its foundations.
I'm being swept into gray, heaving water,
    toward the obscuring mist.

The house has broken from the sandy beach.
I am carried with it beyond the surf,
The loose room, with me inside,
    buffeted by sea and chop.

It was not floating level,
    but reasonably dry.
Cold mist infused the room.
I was splashed by salt-water
    through the glass-less window.
It is not sinking, I thought.
It is not coming apart – not yet.
By no means a sturdy craft,
    nor bulwark against the elements,
    but seems pliable - holding up.
I awaken and come to the terrifying realization:

The ship of my life is under full steam and
mother is not at the wheel!

WE CAN'T TALK   *2/82*

You tell me mundane facts
imbued with other meaning.
I like the part left unsaid,
the *"longing,"* the *"could have been"*
that will not see the light.
Ninety-nine if only's
add only up to zero.

"Why can't we talk?" you say.

"Because we don't understand each other."

"Yes, we do!" you say.

"No, we don't!"

HEAVY, HEAVY
(Divorce day)

2/82

Heavy, heavy
hangs my heart,
my rhythm and my rhyme.
Depressed, I am
at what I see,
and who I am
in time.

SWEET BIRD

2/82

Sweet bird,
where are you
to lift me on your wings?
I need to fly with you
o'er all my cares.

HOPE

2/82

Hope,
I savor you
as a lost child.

Comfort me now.
Lead me
from the pathos
of my present self
into the realm
of lusty life.

FOR MARGE *2/82*

And further, I have this to say,
I am not, nor have I ever been
one for whom roses will not bloom.
For I have learned the ultimate lesson.
The strawberry and grape
are not the same fruit,
yet both taste sweet.
And you are, my dear,
a sweet taste of delight.
Nor is the watermelon,
warm and plump,
a strawberry or grape.
I am not to be fooled.
I shall let knowledge lead me to sunshine.
Tell me that you love my form,
(for I love yours)
that I may be your dearest friend,
and in the telling,
so be led
to sunshine and fresh air.
To warm nocturnal fires,
breathing.

To a rich variety of fruit.
Cover me with lemon-love,
once more, I entreat you.
For we are young,
and yet have time.

CONVERSATION II   *2/82*

*H*ey, der fella, kin I borrow yer-a skooter?

    You wanna borrow my skooter?

Yeah! I wanna borrow yer-a skooter!

    Wha-foah you need-a mah skooter?

Ima gonna catch-a dat squirrel.

    Wha-fo you wanna catcha dat squirrel?

'Cause he swipe-a mah nuts.

    He swipe-a yoah nuts?

He swipe-a mah nuts and-a mah candy.

    Yoa nuts and yoa candy?"

Hurry! Dat squirrel, she's-a gettin' away.

    I tink I saw dat squirrel a-climbin' up-a dat tree.

Oh, No! Dat cannot be!

> *How you gonna chase-a dat squirrel up-a dat tree with-a mah skooter.*

It's a gonna be tuff, but I'ma gonna make it all-a right!

> *Hokay! Here's-a mah skooter. Be ver careful and-a don' a break it.*

I won't. You can-a count on dat!

> *Whoopsee! Lookee him go up-a dat tree afta dat-a squirrel with-a mah skooter. He's pumping away lak-a krazy with-a one foot. Oh! Oh! Look out!*

OOPS! CRASH! BANG! PPHHOOOEEE!

> *Are you-a hurt?*

No! Ah tink am-a goin' ta be Hokay, 'cept for dis beeg-a bump on-a mah noggin'.

> *Hey! De handle ona mah skooter – she's-a broke!*

Ahma sorry 'bout dat.

> *Ann-a de squirrel, she's-a get away!*

Did she take-a mah nuts and-a mah candy?

> *Yeppperie! She took-a yoah nuts ann-a yoa kandy and hide a dem foah de winter in de forest.*

AW! PSHAAW!

WHO'S IN THERE?   *2/82*

If some caring stranger
stopped me on a busy street,
looked deeply into my eyes,
and said,
"Who's in there?"
I would say,
"Wanna go for coffee?"

FATE   *4/82*

Why should I wish to live if I must contend with
        ever-present fate?

For life cannot be lived without impersonal,
        non-caring,
        non-living fate.

I can choose not to live,
        or choose to live,
        side by side,
        with fate.

I was in a state of non-living before I was born.
        I know what non-living is about.
        I am unconscious when I sleep.

Eighteen

But the alive state allows me to be conscious
        of humor, joy, love,
          sadness, pain,
          indifference.

Alive, my cup can be seen as
        half full
        or half empty.

<u>I</u> can give fate its power,
        but I can keep my own.

To me, fate is impersonal,
        does harm as well as good,
        is unaware,
        often appears arbitrary,
        and undependable.

If I give fate its power and keep my own,
        are we then to be adversaries?

No! Because
        fate is not a living being.
        Fate is not a <u>someone</u>.

Fate has no feeling.

Fate does not judge.

Fate has no human characteristics.

Fate just IS!

Fate can lift me to freedom,
        or leave me worse than dead,
        or manipulate me anywhere between.

Fate is not someone who dislikes me.

Fate is not someone against me.

Fate is not someone who cares
> or does not care.

Fate is dead to feeling.

Fate is lifeless and inanimate,
> though it can work
> through the living at times.

Fate has hills and valleys.
> To clamber laboriously upward,
> or to slide gloriously downward.

A person can _use_ fate.

_I_ can use fate.

I can use fate to my own gain.

I can slant fate to my advantage.

I can be opportunistic.

I cannot hurt fate
> because fate is _not_ a living being
> that can be hurt.

I may choose not to injure living beings,
> for to do so, I would injure myself.

But I may do anything I want with fate
> and not feel guilty,
> because fate does not care.
> Fate is incapable of caring.

Eighteen

How I can use fate to my own advantage,
        while not injuring others
        is the question?

I have power.

My power derives its strength from possession
        of mind, body and soul.

I must eat proper food,
        get sufficient exercise,
        sleep regular intervals.

The remainder of time I may <u>use</u> fate
        to my own advantage
        to improve quality of life.

What is the quality of life I'd like to improve?
        What do I want to do with my life,
        functioning without pain?

If I can manipulate fate to my advantage,
        if I have mind-body-soul power,
        how can I use fate for my own gain,
        and what do I wish to gain?

Being alive, accepting ever-present fate,
        allows me to
        fulfill my highest purpose,
        bloom my biggest bloom,
        develop as fate allows.

Who knows, I may get lucky.

YOU SHOULDN'T HAVE DONE WHAT YOU DID   3/83
(A dream)

I've gone to our house
    high on the hill overlooking the sea.
No one is there.
A nice day for waiting
    and falling asleep,
    on cardboard,
    on the grass,
    in the sun,
    in the air.
Snakes, clouds and shadows move.

A truck, arriving, wakens me!
I wonder where I am.
Then I hear a shout.
    "Where do I dump the sauce?"
Uh! Back of the house! OK?
    "Where will the men use their trays?"
There! *(I point.)* OK?
The contractor pulls up to the back of the house
    and tells the driver,
    "Place the sauce evenly around the house."

Looking downward into the bay,
I see commotion in the water.
Army or Navy,
    large amphibian aircraft,
    leaving watery wakes, taking off.
Coast Guard cutters too, and a *"Car"*
    with apparently enormous power,
    full throttle.
They seem to have trouble lifting off.

Plowing through the waves at great speed,
    making huge splashes,
      they lift, skim and plop again into water.
Below us the whole entourage, quite spectacular,
    booms on past with great urgency.

A thief, well-dressed,
    with dark spectacles in thick rims
    is discovered on the site,
    and Bob, a mason friend of mine,
    (to whom I didn't tell the whole truth
    when asked about a job he didn't get,
    but that I gave instead to one of his former workmen)
    appeared and encountered the thief
    and drew a gun on him to hold him at bay.
I thought this heroic.
    Tears welled at the corners of my eyes.

As I turned away,
I noticed the entourage of planes and ships
    had turned inland, having cut a swath,
    and are now zooming in a frenzy
    out of the water,
    up the hill,
    toward our house!
The plane, like a huge car,
    slammed to a stop and men jumped out.
    (Police and Government men.)
They looked for the thick-rimmed glasses man.
The thief held up his hands - caught,
    and let it be known he was the man they sought.
The Police and G-men pulled their guns,
    while Bob had his trained too,
    and when the thief challenged him,
Bob said, *"But then, you shouldn't*
    have done the wrong thing
    that you did!"

I thought this heroic
    in light of Bob being Bob,
    not used to guns and being threatened,
    and risking his life
    during the tense moment before the capture.

"But then, you shouldn't have done
the wrong thing that you did!"
    he had said,
    and then when everything was under control,
    the contractor and I talked to the young police officer.
We discussed how the suspect should have been taken
    if apprehended by a trained policeman.
And then the young officer
    placed his revolver pointed
    into my right shoulder blade.
I was disconcerted,
    apprehensive,
    questioning,
    but in the last,
    he was merely illustrating a point.

And then I saw
    he carried a piece of rather large equipment,
    black and silver,
    a kind of telescopic instrument,
    which allowed him to see clearly,
    yet much larger than ordinary,
    views of distant objects.

He was looking out the window
    and I asked,
    "Can I see too?"
    which he allowed me to do.
I trained the telescope on the distant mountain,
    and clearly saw that which was on the mountain.
    (But not so clearly as I had hoped.)

I thanked the policeman
   and woke up with high blood pressure.

DOCTOR DIFFICULT *3/83*

What have I to say
next to poetical giants,
Yevtushenko, Roethke, Elliot,
having lived a sheltered life?
For I was momma's boy,
doing what I was told,
taking the next step,
doing the expected.

And now I reflect
and wonder what I've done,
and question
how I could be so led.
What shall I do
now that awareness
has flickered
and burst upon me
like the white center
of a dry fire?
I burn,
searching for my power.
I want to be
the power source
and pilot of my ship
broaching adventure's
black wave chop.

I want
is motivation's beginning.

WHEN I DANCE 4/83

I sit on the floor, eyes closed,
    and listen intently to the music
    and try to find those movements
    that are mine –
    that belong only to me.
Those movements that I feel most comfortable
    doing for myself.
I try to express the music,
    but of prime importance,
    is finding the movements
    belonging solely to me.
I find I am most comfortable
    moving in strong contact with the floor.
I like to be vigorous sometimes,
    while at other times
I like to move powerfully and slowly.
I try to be aware of my physical being when I dance,
    down to my fingers and toes.
It is important to stay on balance.
I try to be aware of what I think is good body line,
    but have only what naturally belongs to me.
I do not like to dance
    the way I think others would like me to dance.
That defeats the purpose.

BEYOND RECKONING

Silent,
I sit,
and seeds
of discontent
stir within me.

Breathing fire,
blue ice,
and green water jets,
I bite
tips of trees.

Sighing,
I beg your pardon
for the indifference
that freezes souls,
though you respond
with sunshine,
fresh rain,
and flowers.

Driven into space,
I leap and am lost.

    Spite me,
    spoil me,
    spare me,
    spurn me,
    'Til I die.

A PROTESTATION OF THE HIGHEST ORDER *6/83*
(Following Rick Davidson's powerful and poetic criticisms of the Vietnamese war, I also protest.)

Within this attitude
of mass assassination,
let us begin to realize
the carelessness
of this numbing act
and come, for once,
to terms
with beauty,
joy and thought,
and use our gifts,
intelligence,
and boldness of spirit,
to reject
this murdering
and mayhem
in all its grim
absurdity,
and be resolved
to think instead,
on life,
awareness of women,
and sexual gratification
as the profundity
to best elicit
that self-control
over those basest
interior emotions,
and stop annihilation
in its tracks
before this horrid
specter
eliminates us all.

I cry this out
from my lofty
vantage point
with heartfelt hope
to instigate
within each breast
a will to peace,
nobility and sex.
Let us <u>all</u> hold these thoughts.

Be free!

ON THE DEATH OF DANCER, SUSAN SEIRRA   *6/83*
(Part 1) *(On discovering Susan's body in her Malibu home.)*

Matted dark hair
in a pool of crimson blood
and Susan,
colorful in death
as in life.
And the self questioning.
Could I have saved her?
Was it something I did?
If only I'd read her signs.

And then the seething anger.
After all I'd done.
That last *"Fuck You!"*
was a shot in the head
to those who cared.

And then the reconsideration.
She was, you know,
a frightened child,
almost to death.
Something black and hideous,
(Something we shouldn't know.)
grappled with her soul.

She hadn't ever
been completely loved,
and in horror of the *"other"*
and that final knowing,
pulled the trigger.

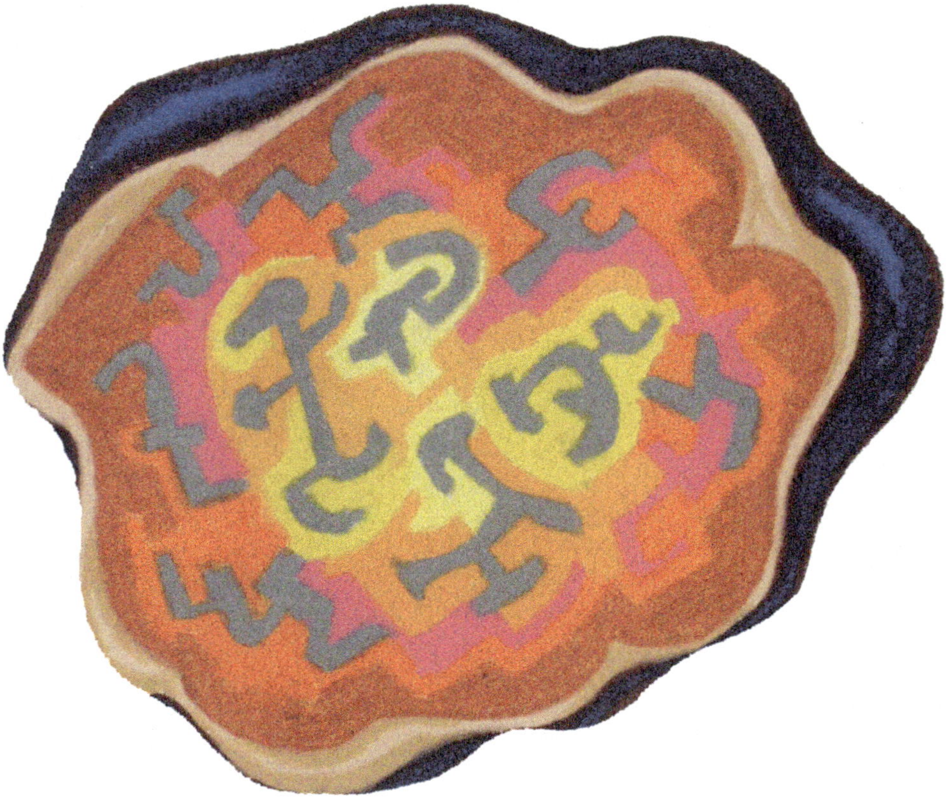

Nineteen

SUSAN'S STUDIO (Part 2)

My time with the studio
was a time of searching
and a time of fighting my way
through some formless mass
threatening to engulf me.
It was also a time of love,
of tenderness,
first sharing,
and rekindling of something very tiny,
akin to hope.

I met Marge, you know,
and a miracle descended
lightly on my shoulders
like a magic cloak
that changed my basic formula
from gray to brilliant white.

But then I broke a family
and questioned why
and how I got so mired,
so stuck,
so helplessly entangled
all by myself.

I remember on the final day
of Susan's six-week class,
nine of us, or so,
ascended the eastern slope
of Bony Ridge Mountain.

In the pre-dawn light
a comet,
Comet West,
briefly passing,
hung still and mysterious
in the deep lavender
of the northern sky.

A breeze caressed our skins
and stirred the chaparral.
It filled our nostrils
refreshingly, as cool water
from a deep spring quenches,
and we felt deeply satisfied,
and reveled in the experience
of a speechless day,
sunrise to sunset.

It was miraculous,
the air,
the mountain,
the sunset,
though in retrospect,
I see the comet
as a _good_ omen.

I was to fall in love.
Susan was to fall in death.

SUSAN'S WAKE (Part 3)

*F*riends assembled at the wake.
Lightly blown rain
rattled on the tin roof.
Thirty sat on the maple floor
in a sharing circle
speaking simple words
of how Susan touched their lives.
*(For her spirit was heavy then
as heavy is it now.)*
At the ceremonies height
a single lightning flash
and a thunder report
rolled and echoed,
retreating down the coast,
followed by silence
and windblown rain
on the old tin roof.

I felt it reasonable
(as comets, love, and suicide)
that this was Susan's sign.
She'd received our love,
and wanting to show her pleasure,
relinquished her dancing space,
with a deep and abiding love,
to us.

HOW I FELT? (Part 4)

*T*his studio is a pain in the ass!
Doesn't that teacher *(Not Deb)*
know I have my office here?
    (The other side of a low wall.)
This is where I work!
    (Jazz-dancing teacher-tenant!
    Her space, but my space too!)
And those dumb, shrill, dance tunes,
designed for idiots
are like to drive me nuts!
I believe I've died and gone to Hell!
    "Turn that music down, you bitch,
    or I'll turn you down!"

I'll never forget the dust.
Oh, yes! Dust!
Grimly, grimily, settling,
constant in its duty.
Ever try to make clean drawings
with dust settling,

minute by minute,
second by second?
Slowly sifting dust
settling on your paper,
while the monotonous beat
of innocuous tunes
scratches your eardrums at 90 DB?
DB means decibel as well as dumb-bell.

Well, move out then!
Eventually, I did.
That fricking dance studio
was a pain in the ass,
and so was the building.

DANCING WITH DEB (Part 5)
(After Susan's death, Debby Dorland Feltman took over as dance teacher. Improvisational dance classes continued.)

But if I was unhappy with the building,
that doesn't include Deb.
DEBRA DORLAND FELTMAN.
Our Deb!
The enchantress.
Her magic transformed the hell-hole
into a wonderland.
I'm not sure Deb's aware
this building's falling down.
Its rotten at the foundation.
When the wind blows,
the termites hold hands.

I've seen snakes in here
feeding on the mice
who were feeding on roaches!
Its old!
Its cold!
Its unfit for habitation!
History be damned!
This place is dead,
it just hasn't been buried yet!

But Deb didn't know.
She still doesn't know.
She saw a dance studio,
and with her special lantern
cast a magic charm,
turned this pumpkin-space
into a chariot
with golden wheels
and six fine horses.
All the frogs
became princes.
I should know.
I was a frog.
Into this building
    of ancient gloom,
      she brought acceptance,
      flexibility,
      planning, imagination,
      caring and diligence,
      improvisation and joy,
      judgement and sincerity,
      and loving leadership,
      and under her spell,
      her dancers saw it too.

    Red and green shadows
    cross-armed on the wall,
    finger waving and forearms

reaching, as healthy plants,
for nourishment and life.
Imaginary spaces,
tunnels, precipices,
cubistic and balloon shapes,
cones and whirling spaces
of dancing movement,
dazzling to the eye.

Group-follow focus,
concentration,
doing everybody's dance.
Expressing admiration,
creative innovation,
mutual admiration
of each to every member
of the group.

Multiplicity of sounds
rebounding in the room.
Jarrett, Copeland, Jarre.
Animated human forms
reflecting every mood.

Slow-posed mirror dance,
thrust of leg and elbow,
open finger wiggles,
gesture of the hip and thigh,
fascinating shapes.
Whirling,
kaleidoscopic
view of dizzy lights.
Feel of hand in hand,
as round and round,
the group is still,
and the room flashes by.

Or Debby does her creature dance,
somersaulting backwards,
thrusting her hips,
then her lips,
knees and elbows waving,
scratches her butt,
rolls, leaps, falls,
and assumes her creature pose.

Or Dirk
parts a rent
in a canvas womb,
and with determination,
decision, steps right through
to freedom,
adventure.

Marge, arm low,
turns into an upward spiral,
increasing her speed,
bursts in spinning,
and fills the space,
light as a bird,
then settles to the floor
in silence and reflection.

But most of all
the hugging clump
of dancers and affection.
The generosity of spirit,
the caring energy projected
from each to other.
The unifying energy of love,
the magic of Deb and her dancers
is the studio, for me,
and though this space
may assume another shape,

I shall go where my dancers go,
and as for this space,
I wish God-speed
and trust to memory.

DANCE   6/83

On the floor stretching,
like a knotted rubber band,
kicking its kinks,
I take floor-turns,
then crunch into a monkey.
From my primate pose
I swing my arm,
and leap to my feet.
Then begin
my ancient moves
in effort
and in speed
increasing,
feel my heartbeat coming
fast and clear,
inhaling deep
and breathing.
My blood is warm,
like mother's milk.
My body sings to my heart
and the combination:
Dance.

SEARCH

Hello, Doctor.
> *Hello, what can I do for you?*

I have a question.
> *Ask, please.*

How can I protect myself from knowing my intrinsic worthiness?
> *A good question, my son.*

Can you shed some light, Doctor, on how I'm to protect myself?
> *Why do you ask?*

I don't know if I should love myself or not.
> *Who is yourself?*

I don't know. That's why I'm here.
> *How can I help you decide whether you love yourself if you can't tell me who yourself is?*

I thought there might be some other way.
> *Well, you could develop a neurosis.*

I already have one.
> *How does it affect you?*

Insomnia, nervousness, high blood pressure, indigestion.
> *I'm so sorry.*

Just what is a neurosis, Doctor?
> *The basis of neurosis is ignorance or lies you tell yourself to protect you from knowing the truth of your worthiness.*

My neurosis doesn't seem to be doing the job.
> *You could develop a new symptom that might take your mind off having to learn who you are so you could decide if you are love-worthy or not.*

I'm practically dead from the four symptoms I have, Doctor, I would prefer not to have to add another one.
> *Why don't you look in to who you are? Maybe you will be pleasantly surprised or at least OK in your own eyes.*

The risk is too great.
> *You mean, down deep, you suspect there's a 70-30 chance you're not worthy of your own affection?*

Yep! That's it! The risk is too great!
> *Have you ever thought of becoming obsessed with Jesus or joining an Hari-Krishna group or some kind of cult where some authority figure would absolve you of all your supposed or real sins and would love you even if in your own eyes you were still not worthy?*

I'm not the religious type.
> *How about other forms of self-destruction? How about doing dangerous stunts for TV? If you don't get killed, you could make lots of money. You could blow things up.*

No! No! No! I just want to feel good and live out my life in a normal constructive manner. Perhaps even contribute to world harmony, or something.
> *How about suicide? There are new painless ways ...*

Sometimes I feel like it. I usually don't feel <u>that</u> bad. Just moderately punky.
> *You know, Sol, I care about you.*

You do?
> *Of course I do.*

You got any degrees or anything?
> *I'm a Doctor. I have taken special training in my field. I'm competent. It says so right on my license. Why do you ask about degrees?*

What does it mean to me if a moderately competent Doctor cares about me?
> *You mean if I had more degrees; if I was really somebody, like a Pope or a President and cared about you, then you would feel better about yourself and your neurotic symptoms would go away and you would begin to live a life of self-fulfillment and joy?*

Sounds kind of ridiculous, when you put it that way, Doctor.
> *I think you needed your mother and father to love you, don't you?*

I wished mother had loved me.
> *Didn't your mother love you?*

She said she did.

Didn't you believe her?
I guess I did.
Why are you being vague?
It's just the *way* she said it.
You mean if she told you she loved you in just the right way, you might have believed her?
Am I being too picayune?
I don't think so. Where is your mother now?
Des Moines.
Why don't you call her?
I called her last week. She's into her life and doesn't seem to care what I do anymore.
You still hope to get her to tell you she loves you in just the right way?
She never changes.
How long have you been trying to get her to say she loves you in just the right way?
For years now.
All your life?
All my life.
Sounds like you haven't changed either.
That's different.
What do you mean, different?
Mothers are suppose to love you in just the way you need them to love you.
Is that written down somewhere?
Are you trying to trap me? You're just trying to trap me! If you continue to pursue this line with me, I shall have to cancel our appointment!
Do so, if you feel the need.
Well, watch it!
Sorry.
You don't care!
Yes, I do.
No you don't.
Yes I do.
Yeah? How much?

A lot!
You liar! You don't know me that well. I just came in here today. I've known you for about a half hour, and already you say you care about me. You lie!
I care about the human species.
Oh? Now I'm not human?
*Of course you're human. I care about you even though
I've only known you for about a half hour.*
Yeah? How much?
We've been through that.
But you've never answered it to my satisfaction.
I love you one hundred percent.
You do?
Yes, I do.
I still don't feel good.
*Don't you think it's about time you faced the real issues?
Why don't you do some introspection,
find out who you really are so you can decide
if you are worthy of your own love?*
OK. I guess I'll try.
Thank you.
How do I do that?

END OF THE ROAD   *6/83*

The runner runs,
head down.

The pavement
flashes beneath his feet.
with perfect vision.

His thoughts arrive one by one
in order of importance.

He machinates.
He dwells.
He broods.

He holds anger,
while dashing pavement
recedes beneath his feet.
The runner's gaze lifts.
The road extends,
and narrows in the distance,
straight to the top of a low rise,
and beyond.
The end of the road is death.
The struggle of the run is life.

The hills in between the runner
and the end of the road
rise and fall
are difficult or easy,
but the end is the same.
The more effort he exerts,
the faster he arrives
at the top of the rise,
or the end of the road.

INDESCRETION   *6/83*
(Dictionary poem #1: fustrum, dauphin, friable, Mergansers.)

*F*inally I saw her!
We held discourse,
but I discovered
she'd been indiscreet.

She had always been
imprudent,
rash,
in a way that endeared her to men.

To look at her
was to exempt her
from punishment.

I was reminded
of her mother's shape,
like a <u>fustrum</u>.
(remainder of a truncated cone)

Lord how I lied.
I even tried discord,
for our discussion
was confused noise.

Then I learned
she was a <u>dauphin.</u>
(heir to the crown of France)
I fell to my knees
in tribute.

Returning home,
I thought to make

myself productive.
I worked on a <u>friable</u> cake
(easily crumbled)
until the chicken
was frickaseed.

I never saw her again,
but heard
she'd crossed to Wales
on a tuna boat
to live among
the <u>Mergansers.</u>
(fish eating ducks)

FOOD FOR THE ANCIENT GREEK   *8/83*
(Dictionary Poem #2: hoplite, jackstay, patagium, scones.)

*T*he ancient Greek <u>hoplite</u>
(heavy-armed foot-soldier)
ate the rough skin
of a File-fish.

His stomach
whipped and tugged
like a <u>jackstay</u>
(for fastening sails)
loose in the wind.

He prefers
the rarer meat
of the flying squirrel,

and could catch him, too,
were it not
for the patagium,
(the skin between the legs)
allowing the giant leaps.

He settles for
indurate scones
(a cake of meal)
baked on a griddle,
grown hard with time.

LISA RUSCHEK   *8/83*
*(Dictionary poem # 3: metronymic, parvenu, Reebok,
damascene, soubrette, Veda, telergy.)*

Lisa Ruschek,
whose name was metronymic
(being derived from her mother's side)

acquired a fortune,
and lived it up
a full time parvenu.
(a newly rich upstart)
She jetted to Africa,
southern tip,
and rode a Reebok
(light gray antelope)
just for the fun.

Returning,
she dabbled in damascene,

(inlaid iron with decorative gold)
and drinking and partying.

She was a frivolous woman,
a soubrette,
(acting a pert young woman)
if you please,
until saturated.

Studying the Veda,
(sacred literature of the Hindus)
her interests broadened,
but it was not until
she claimed telergy
(mental influence of others)
that she was taken seriously.

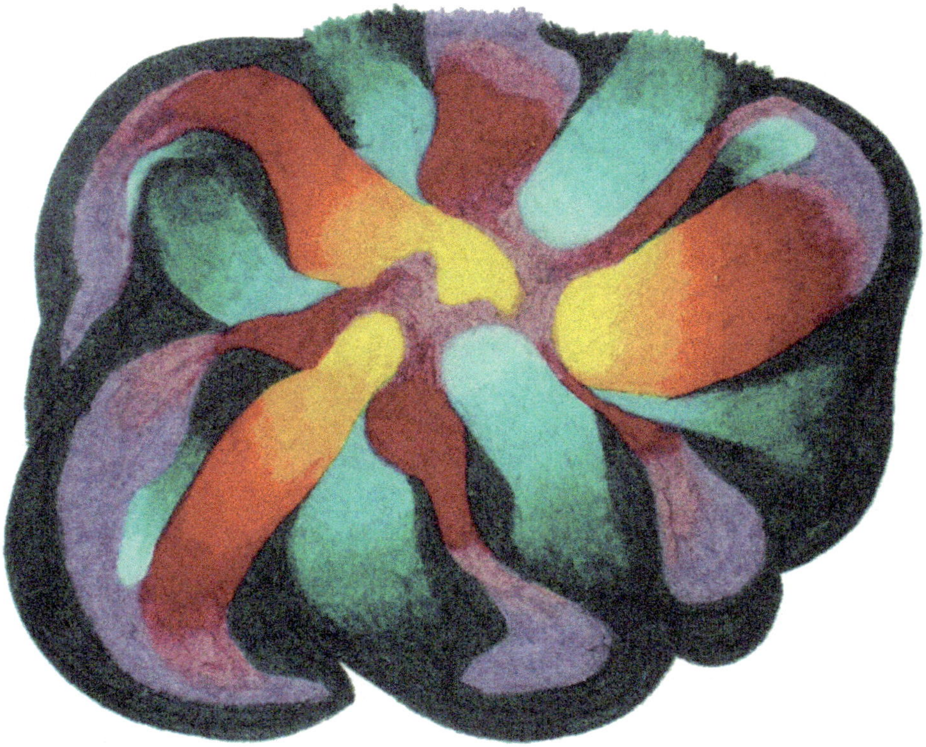

Twenty

ROARK *8/83*
(Dictionary poem # 4: telegony, Tebbad, lycanthropy. nooligist, Heptaglot, Wonga, Gorgonzola, Poult-de-sole, gassoon.)

Roark,
adolescent son
of Madelien and Peter,
was much like
the mysterious Obidiah,
Madalien's first husband.

This <u>telegony</u> surfaced
*(the supposed transmission
of characters of one sire*

*to the offspring subsequently born
to other sires by the same female)*
during the Tebbad,
(sandstorm or simoon)
that periodically sweeps
Central Asia.

He developed
lycanthropy,
(imagining himself a werewolf)
as had Obidiah.
Peter, nonplussed,
but a noologist of repute,
(one skilled in the art of reasoning)
documented his observations
in Heptaglot,
(a book in seven languages)
subsequently debunked
in Australia
and fed to the Wonga's
(large pidgeons)
Roark,
who never fully recovered,
took to wolfing
great quantities
of Gorgonzola,
(Italian cheese)
and wearing
Poult-de-sole,
(a silk fabric from France)
heavily corded,
and eventually became
quite the continental gassoon.
(young lad)

INSTANT SPACE   *11/83*

*F*ull well
the evening moon
lifts from the rim
of time's cavern.
Iridescent,
the night flowers
leap on tall stems
multi-piercing
the rich field grass
lying straight
between the brown
trunk grove
and shimmering sea.
Reclining
in the wilderness
of his particular
planet, I muse
on why and wherefore
I drifted here,
you see,
and as well
would have drifted there.
For the sparkling universe,
thick with wonder,
is my instant space,
and I live, eternal,
content to be.

POSSIBLE TO LIVE

Look not,
but thy fragile self
is in the fitful night.
Hear not
the shrill, black winds
that freeze the stars.
See not
the hellish pinnacles
that rip the sky.
Lower thine eyes
and wish for *nice*.
Think on
wild roses, radiant
in fragrant fields,
sultry violets
and pansies, bright.
Partake
of that which feeds
upon itself.
Dull eye, slack jaw.
Toad on the rock,
Man on the earth.
    Hear not!
    See not!
But know it possible
    to live
a somewhat
palatable life.

I WRITE *1/84*

He sits with full stomach
    pressing against his belt.
    A bulk.
    A hulk.
A regular Mickey Markum
who thinks with his brain,
    in vain.
Rubbery, sticky, gray matter
    slumps, tired,
against his cranium bone.
    He mopes
in the wildest of hopes,
    and waits
for a glimmer,
    a flicker,
or even a warm spot
in the congealing jell
of thickened thoughts
that might hold promise
    for a thought
    to be thunk.
A think to to be thank.
    He sat,
    was fat,
    and thunk
He thinks and stinks
(He thank and stank.)
His brain, lost as wood.
    Hopeless!
Dead and forgotten.
    Rotten!
Let us pray.

YOUPA GOUPA
(Discovery of soup.)

Youpa goupa
Gum de Soupa!

Neanderthal man
smilingly rose
loving his nose
aroma wafting
from sister Lowes
garden groves.

Ug-wump, tooey!
Itsall gooey!
Whatsis? Whatsis?
Tastesall fooey!

Youpa goupa
Gum de Soupa!

Whatsis? Whatsis
Gum de Soupa?

Gum de Soupa's
youpa – doupa
tatees's, corn,
t'matees, bean,
from stems is torn,
trone in de watah.
Can't you seen?

Yu good Goupa!
Giv mor Youpa
Gum-de-Soupa!

But you sed whatsis,
tastesall fooey?!
Gimme tatees, corn
t'matees bean,
from stems is torn
or I be mean!

Youpa Doupa
Gum de Soupa!

THE SEED 4/84

As the seed,
given the gift of life,
returns it by blooming,
so like humans.

Our spirit, like the flower,
longs to fulfil itself.

Not born to suffer,
our actions must spring from desire
to do that which gladdens our hearts,
makes us feel free.

We are our best when growing,
when fulfilling our longing,
when following the path we like best.

Taking our unique gift,
our principal temperament,

our special ability,
we risk it,
correct errors,
grow,
and fulfill our spirit's longing.
Not to be acted upon,
we must act upon.

YOU GOT ME THINKING *5/84*

*I*f reality is your friend,
not to pursue it
is to opt for fantasy,
which results in knowing less,
and being less aware,
which is a move toward
unconsciousness,
and ultimately, death.

To pursue reality
is to opt for knowing,
which is to become more aware,
which is a move toward
higher consciousness,
and a richer life experience.

People opt for fantasy
out of fear of knowing,
which means they are
protective
of that which they don't wish to know.

To move from Fear-protection to Love-learning
requires moving through pain issues,
yet expressed in rich learning.

EXTRAS *7/84*

Which Record for You?

Doug Rucker Sings
    or
Beethoven's Fifth played at 45 speed?

Possums

It is possum time in the old corral,
and it is possums on parade.
Let's hear it for the possums!
Big, small, medium.
Like burglars,
they scare you in the night.

You Know

It is easier to be polite when you're rich.

Don't be Afraid

*D*o not be afraid.
It is only I, the
MUGWUMPIWILLIWORT!

From the Shore, the Roar

*D*own the lanes of window panes,
in the store for more.
Down the shoot came a boot,
from the shore, the roar.

Thinking-birds Dog
(Bird builds nest on dog's head)

*D*og is but god
in reverse.
Nor do I judge
the unique,
nor mistrust
nature's divine law,
but accept
that which exists
beyond understanding,
and observe
the carefully laid plans
of the thinking-bird's dog.

UNRELATED THOUGHTS **8/84**
(Automatic writing poem.)

I grasped the shell,
translucent in its swirls,
and flung it into night.

How crisp the air.
How clear the sight.
Those ageless stars
of flaming might,
transfixed and cursed,
free or blessed,
am I made to live,
or doomed to die?

*I cast myself on luminescent stones
and dreamed.*

Baby shoots of grass
pierce the crumbled earth.

The fragrant night,
jasmine, honeysuckle, broom-weed,
and then the floating sounds
from a lavender realm beyond.

Mother puts mullberries in a bowl.
They grew between the curb and sidewalk.
Full steam, my ship of life is under way.
Mother is <u>not</u> at the wheel.

Though concealment was my aim,
they saw me all the same.

The sweet lake breeze,
through the window,
rustles desk-papers,
freshens my room.

Rays refracting from a diamond sun,
spear the mist of early morn.

I contemplate my navel.
Where's the lint?

LEAVES IN THE GARDEN 8/84
(Poem #1 from <u>A Book of Everyday Stuff</u>)

Leaves in the garden,
brown and dry,
crackle
like sweet milk from mother's breast.
"Let me know the truth,"
said the mother bear.

Here in the soft rains,
the night resounds
from shore to shore,
echoes,
mountain to rill.

Haven't we ...
at some time ...
ever ...?

I think of ecstasy
in the night
by firelight
while fireflies
breathe the soft perfume,
and elephants and snails,
possums and giraffes,
listen and dream in the night.

The soft, soft,
softly falling,
the streak, the streaking,
the window crying
for my lost,
my losing ...

I WISH   **8/84**
(Poem #2 from <u>A Book About Everyday Stuff</u>.)

I wish
    and the wish beckons me,
dark to light,
    as the bean tendril,
blind of eye,
    yet parts the darkened soil,
D
R
O
P
S

to nourishment
and requisition,
    so desired,
    so craved,
    so necessary
to catalyze
    soul and body.

I wish,
and the wish quickens me,
slow to fast,
    for that momentary rush,
that infinitesimal
    flash of light
in time's immense cavern,
    I own
that for which I'd yearned,
    before I'm plunged
into reality's grim abyss.

I wish,
    and the anticipation of,
perhaps obtaining,
    gladdens my heart,
and I am lifted on
    wings of ...

THE WINDS THEY CAME A-WHISTLING 8/84
(Poem # 3 from <u>A Book About Everyday Stuff</u>.)

The winds
they came a-whistling
through the corners
of my mind,
and blew
the living daisies
like a ripened
melon rind.
I sat upon my shoelace,
looking for a sock,
and then a simple melody
approached,
or was it really *"rock."*
I looked at her,
she looked at me,
I scrutinized her eye,
and then she gave me
ecstasy,
a piece of pecan pie.
I turned to her
said, *"Thank you ma'am,"*
and bowed my lovin' head.
To think she cared so much for me ...

(Aaaah! - I think I'll go to bed!)

THINK ON, FAIR LILY *8/84*
(Poem #4 from A Book About Everyday Stuff.)

*T*hink on, fare night Lily,
you of the darkened forest,
radiant near your stone,
delicate in your fragrant power.
Think on me.
Think on thee.
Think on dreamy
spaces of tomorrow
and of yesterday.
Think on passing of your stone,
mountain to boulder to rock
to pebble to sand to ether.
Passing of stones,
worn by the winds,
and insect trails,
and dewdrops.

Stones, worn by eons of fogs,
and myriad rays of sunlit days.

Think on stones,
shrunk by trillions
of shadows passing,
of starlight lights
on moonless nights,
and cat's claws,
and crow's caws.

Fair Lily
of the brilliant stones,
think on worn stones ...

Twenty

'dem stones,
'dem stones,
'dem <u>dry</u> stones
and here is de word of de Lawd.

EXTRAS 8/84
Poem #5 from <u>A Book About Everyday Stuff</u>.)

I Have a ...

I have a ...,
and the solid,
too, too, heart
of the wood-nut tree,
spreading and closing
as if to the wind,
reveled ...,
and then as if to ...,
and the heaving
and swelling night,
and the coming and going
of the multi-colored stars,
the bird,
high on the wind,
wings stretching,
black an steady,
arched ...

Born of the Air

Born of the air,
I rise
on shimmering heat
and glide through billows
and pillows
of clouds,
seeking a feeling,
an ethereal ceiling,
dense as a pomegranate,
rich as a marmoset.
Potency
fills my still,
and I drink passion,
'til tipsy and daring,
I love.

I SAVOR *8/84*
(Poem #6 from A Book About Everyday Stuff.)

I savor
the lustrous light
of self-aggrandizement,
where nothing is holier
than to say,
"How-de-do, muchacho!"

Basking, as I do,
like the sunfish,
in the easy warmth

of self-approval,
I stun the world!
Pow! Pow! Pow!

Be aware,
my universe.
Feel the heartbeats
ringing across
the wheat-fields,
the lily-ponds,
the lilac gardens,
filling the voids
of loneliness,
despair ...
Ding! Dong! Ding! Dong!

Pity not
the lowly me,
for I am as great,
and grand,
and noble,
as any dog can be.
"How-de-do! Muchacho!"

SOMETIMES RAIN 8/84

*T*wilight.
Dave 2,
Doug, 6.
Father, 36,
arms circling both.

Summer evenings,
sitting on grass,
backs pressed flat
    on white
    clapboard
    house
in comfortable Saturday, clothes
watching *heat lightning*
over wasted fields,
rumble and play
above Chicago.
Occasionally it would metamorphose
into a full blown storm advancing
and real lighting would drill the earth
in powerful bolts.
Sometimes rain.

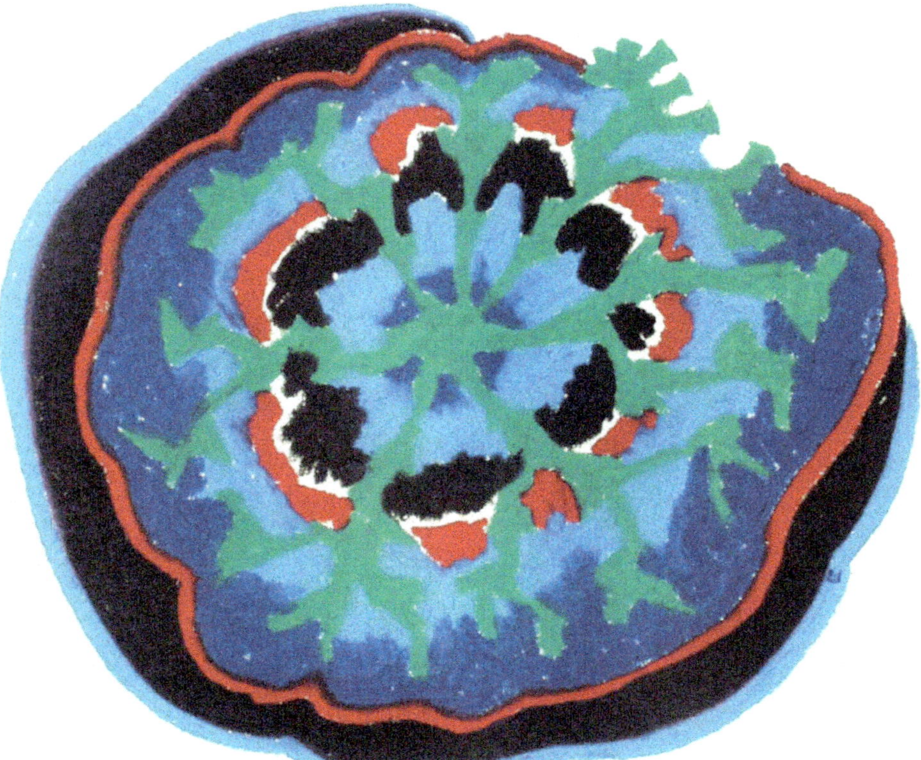

Twenty-one

FIRST MEMORY 9/84?

I am four,
standing stuck,
bundled,
unable to move.
Wading puddles seemed like the perfect idea,
under the gray overcast of a late afternoon
in March, '32.

A chilling gale
gusted out of the north across the Illinois planes,
swooped over the little town of Lombard,
west of Chicago,

whipped the winter bark off trees,
and stung my little cheeks
rosy red.

Head down, trudging home,
I almost walked into it.
A slushy old mud puddle,
oblong and black,
freezing, mucky old hole,
surrounded by the mushy snow.

It looked so inviting,
How could I not slip,
hip deep,
into it,
until the frigid water seeped in my stockings,
and thrills whipped my spine.

My booties were stuck!

It got dark.

Time passed.

I struggled.

I was cold
and frightened,
until a distraught
and pregnant mother
discovered me,
pulled me,
shoeless,
from the mire.

IMAGINED MEMORY *9/84*

*T*hree years old,
I reached up,
grabbed the big knob of the basement door
with both fat hands,
and turned.

The door swung back over the stairs,
cold air rushed up from the blackness,
past my eyes, my skin,
my raising hair.
I looked down the steps,
and saw through the vent
a fire in the furnace door.

It made a feeble light.
I grasped the railing overhead
and made my way downstairs.
The flames through the vent were exciting.
I watched for a long time.
When I was done,
I turned back to the room.
The darkness was impenetrable
except for a coal pile
that sloped steeply to a high casement window.
I climbed the pile,
coal slipping and tumbling.
I breathed coal dust.
I was dirty and uncomfortable,
and thought about going back.

The door slammed shut.
It was darker.
I was frightened,
and breathed more rapidly.

Coal dust in my mouth,
I climbed the pile
to get to the window.

The room was black.
I began to cry.
I was cold.
No one came.

I crouched on the coal,
No one came.

PARTS OF ME I'LL KEEP   *9/84*

Parts of me I'll keep
as they pass through me freely.
I'll keep rainstorms, comfortable beds,
a quiet body, children, friends, a mate,
drawing, writing, dancing,
clouds, snow, leaves, trees, wind-blowing
and many other things.

Parts of me I'll try to lose.
Those portions that get stuck inside
rather than passing through.

I'd be like a clogged pipe,
matted filter,
shorted circuit.

Bad things get stuck.
Friction builds up.

The organism panics!
I heat up!
I build a dangerous charge!
I begin to die with stresses and strains!
I must allow life to pass through,
(good and bad)
unstuck.
So I'll be nourished by life,
not destroyed by life.

MATCHING STARS 9/84
(A dream)

I am outside.
It is twilight.
I take points of light,
like diamonds,
and arrange them on the ground.

Two stars *(points)* are larger
and have special power,
and so I arrange them
in such a position
it will strengthen the lower *"cross"*
of the design,
so that when I pick it up,
it will not fall apart.

When I have the diamonds,
or points, properly arranged,
and the real stars have come out,

I grasp the design,
(it has edges that are graspable)
and hold it up to the sky.

I try to match my design
with <u>real</u> stars.

I try to get my diamond design
to fall in exact sync
with the real stars.

I'm compelled to get them
to match up.

When they do,
something wonderful will happen.
Two neighbors come out
from nearby homes
and watch me do this.

They think I'm strange,
a poetic, philosophic,
sort of fellow.

I sense they approve of me,
and think of me as somehow, special.
I feel their warmth and respect,
even though I suspect
their skepticism and humor
toward me.

Yet, it is important I match my stars
with the real stars, and I continue,
though my arms are tired
from holding them up.

I cannot get more than one or two stars
to match my design.

Then I think ...
"Where the stars can see a gorgeous view of the daytime!"
This poetic thought wakes me up.

EXTRAS   9/84

Sunflower

*T*he sunflower grows
to the tips of it's toes.

My Reflection

*M*y reflection
is perfection.

My True Love's Nose

*Y*ellow was my true loves nose.
I met her where the morning glory grows.

TV Set

I never met
a T V set
I didn't like.

The Ocean

The ocean
is motion.

No Choice

Violets
have no choice.

Drying Dew

The dew is dying,
while it's drying.

To Know the Leaf

To know the leaf,
just ask the dew.

Pickles

Green pickles
break dry mouths.

Cat's Fleas

My cat has fleas.
My dog pees.
Desperation time
for a rhyme.

NOTHING *9/84*

*Y*oung fellow
digs hole,
boards across,
makes *"hut."*

Inside,
through boards,
sunlight slits
cross bare legs.

Old fellow,
in study,
lies on couch,
face to ceiling.

Wrist to brow,
makes dreams.
Through blinds,
sunlight slits
cross chest.

And the cheery tree
flowering,
and the green cherries,
and the yellow cherries,
ripening,
and the red cherries,
ripe and juicy,
and the eating,
and the jarring of the jaw
on hard pits.
Why is this interesting?
It's not - unless you're me.

What has this to do with a reader?
Nothing.

A DREAM - Can it be True?   9/84

*H*air follicles bristle on the back of my neck.
My spine tingles, I begin weeping.

I lay on the bed
where I had been sitting,
tears streaming from the corners of my eyes,
in a tense state of recollection.
I fall into fitful sleep and dream.

*(He sits on the right side of the sofa, and I face him,
his head against the window obscuring his face.
It is sundown, and he has come to give me the estimate.
He, in white shirt, trim socks, dark pants,
with scratch-pad or clip-board.)*

After pleasantries, I ask him for his bid.
I expect it to be $100,000.00.
He answers $400,000.00.

I am shocked!
I say nothing to him.

I am in a state of disbelief!

I study him to see if he's bluffing.

He is silent.

He doesn't retract his statement.

I can't believe it!

I search my mind for meaning.

Could the price be correct?

Have I overlooked anything?

Are my drawings in error?

Is it my fault?"
He holds firm.

Through the window,
two flashes of lightning.

After a short length of time,
two more flashes.

They punctuate the happening in our conversation,
but I can't remember what, or if.
I hear no thunder.

FISH LAKE 9/84

Tall oak trees.
Violent thunder storms.
Sleeping on the screened porch.
Mosquitoes at night.

Early morning mist on water.
Soft ca-cooing of the dove.
Fishing poles.
Row-boat rides.
Sounds of oars.
Humid afternoon sun.
Dragging your feet.
Still water.
Bow cutting through lily-pads.
Frogs, snakes, snapping turtles.
Reeds, cat-tails, fireflies at twilight.
Soft, swampy earth.
Stinging nettles.
blue-gills, rock bass, crappies.
Garfish, bull-heads, sunfish.
Red-winged blackbirds.
Hot, sandy road to Blackman's.
Bate, fishing lures, Mary Jane's.
Popcicles, Guess-Whats, Ne-Hi drinks.
Rancid peanut butter on soft white bread.
Hot-dogs roasted over open fires.
Corn, baked in burnt husks.
Marshmallows.

AN EQUALITY   *9/84*

That this too, too,
in the infinite
speeding universe,
infiltrating all,
and the space in between,
black and cold,

that we,
lost in this infinite,
roam toward,
or away from,
but always with speeding.
Yet the divine rhythm,
flowing, pulsing,
as a bright heart
beats with love,
excitement,
enthusiasm,
lusting for life,
and the curious-ness
that this,
and the infinitely expanding stars,
and the blackness,
and the separateness,
and the close beat of the heart,
are one and the same.

I WRITE   9/84

Nothing
comes to mind,
just blank paper.
No pencil,
or pen,
or chalk,
or stick,
or other thing.
Just blank paper

growing in size
before my eyes,
lighter, brighter,
filling the screen
of my own minds eye
with white and glowing,
deceptively growing,
blank - blank - paper.

Suddenly!
From the air
I have my pen.
It flies to my fingers.
Aha! I shall write!
I lift it just so.
I will tell you everything!
Gloriously, greatly,
all will know!

Surcharged
with feeling,
with intensity, meaning,
my eager black pen-point
now presses the paper.
I move my hand.
I write.
No ink!

TELEPHONES *10/84*

Like watching a pot
that refuses to boil,
so an idea,
openly coaxed,
will never come out,
but shyly, defiantly,
clings to its hiding place,
wedging its tiny frame
into a hole.
Hounded and horrified,
acts like a mole
when poked with a stick.
Come on little thought,
idea or feeling,
I know you're concealing
a fine personality.
Open up, show me
you are freewheeling.
I watch like a watch-pot
for some little sign,
emotion or insight
to make my heart pound,
when glory-be,
just as I'm turning around,
guess what comes haltingly
out of the ground?
No sudden movements, now.
Keep very still.
Just play it cool, now,
I may have my will.
Breathlessly waiting,
like capturing a fawn,
the little thought-fellow's

beginning to dawn ...,
RRRiiinnnggg!
Hello! Hello?
Is that you, George?
This is Marge.
Is Janet home?
I'm at the market.
What kind of Jell-O?
George?
Hello?
Hello?

I LISTEN FOR RUMBLINGS 10/84

I feel the humid atmosphere
clinging to my skin.
I perspire clean water,
and breath heavy air.

I sit in my chair
observing bark of trees,
and dripping leaves,
low-slung clouds,
and droplet crowds,
clinging to the eaves.

I listen for rumblings
of late summer thunder,
and wonder at living things
that gnaw at roots
of long green grass,

and baby sucker shoots,
naive beneath the sky.

I see violets leaping
on too-tall stems,
and ivy tendrils creeping
on the back-yard fence.

The vegetable world is dense,
and I dream on these things,
on dragon-fly wings,
sleeping dogs,
and what fall brings.

ODE TO GLOOM 11/84

I could feel the wind
on that moonless night.

The stars refused
to mark the sky.

When she did appear,
the moon dripped blood,

and wore gauze
across her face.

A leaf on a gale
blown from a tree

flew to a grave
in a forgotten place.

The grasses, creaking,
bowed to the ground,

hissing, shrieking,
a terrible sound.

In dim,-dumb, wakefulness
a coasting shark

with pig-little eyes,
disappears, quietly,

massive, eternal,
into the dark.

THE WOLF AND I   12/84

*T*he close growl of a wolf.
The yellow, slit eye, calm gaze of the wolf.
The raised hair on the back of the neck.
The snarl and white teeth,
yellowing nearer the gum-line,
vivid, as a dream!
God, I hate that mouth!

And the patterned,
thick fur on the collar of his neck.
"What is it you want, wolf?"

I meet that steady look,
the energy pulsating outward, relaxing.
The intensity pulsating, relaxing.
Go away from me!

A low growl!
Crouching, I wait.
"What are you waiting for, wolf?"
Will you eat me now, or while I sleep?
Will you chase me in the misty dawn,
through fresh green grasses,
wet with dew, through long primeval grasses,
with razor edges that lacerate my shins
as I run, headlong, in panic?

Shall I briefly register your haunches
flex and bunch beneath that luxurious fur
on your hind-quarters, as you run
pursuing your prey *(me)* to our final trapping place?
And with all avenues of escape exhausted,
shall I then turn on my great fear and,
surprised at finding something within me
I knew not I had. Shall I turn,
snarling, to meet your face -
face to face?
Turn and meet your yellow teeth, my death,
as they clench and grip, and rip,
hot around my throat?
And shall you win, then,
or shall I somehow prevail,
summoning every inner resource?

Might I not get bigger than I am,
under such a threat,
and become, myself, a threat,
shoot the energy, *(my will)*
so forcefully from my heart and chest,
arm and teeth,
my-newfound strength
shall penetrate your hide,

like x-rays,
that dampen your will,
sending chills of your own fear descending in waves
down your yellow spine?

Or shall we clash in mortal battle as equals,
each determined to prevail?
And what of our courage, you and I?

Shall you be defeated, or I?

I'll wrench your limb from it's socket,
as you chew my forearm.
I'll plunge my fist past your yellow teeth,
feeling your gagging tongue
into your windpipe,
so your victim chokes you.
You'll roll back your eyes,
and, claws extended,
whip and undulate your body
in a frantic effort to free yourself.
And wolf, with slit eyes,
focused, intent,
locked in steady contact on mine,
who watches us struggle?

Does our maker sit,
white-robed,
enthralled upon the spectacle?
Enjoying the passion of his *(our)* conflict?
Does he sit alone on his golden throne
(with unselected angels)
conducting a test of wills-to-survive?
Or is there no maker?

All gone home.
(An empty throne)
No one watching.

Bleachers bare,
while we combat for no reason?

Is there no way to make peace, you and I,
yellow, slit-eyed wolf,
with determined gaze,
fixed eyes , steady, on mine?

If so, we must relax simultaneously
and find mutual trust.

If so, what an invincible team we'd be!

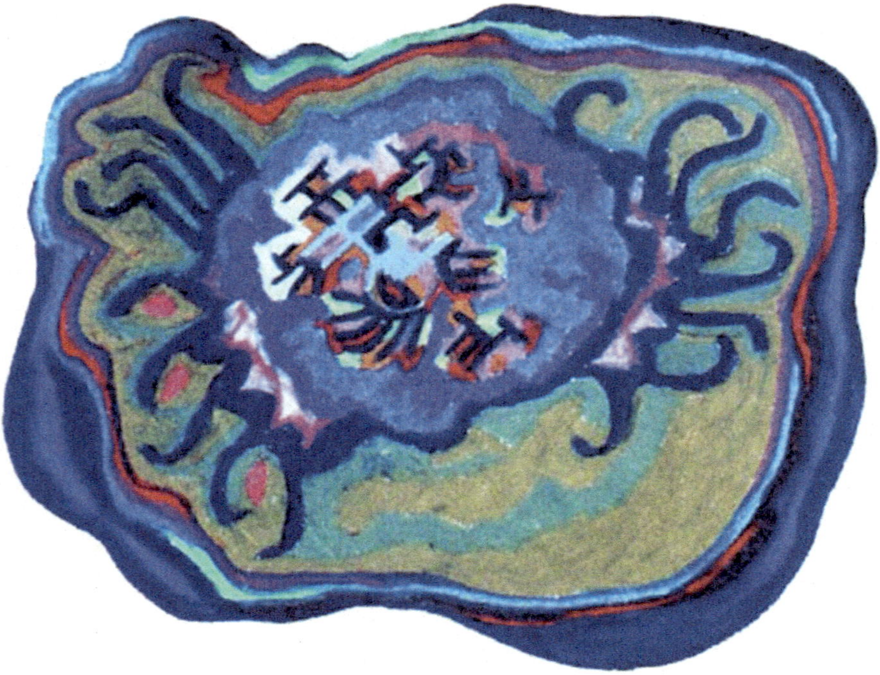

Acknowledgements

I especially want to thank Helane Freeman for translating my work into InDesign, and negotiating the book through ISBN, Federal Copyright laws, and a listing in Amazon.

I wish to express my gratitude to Ron Munro for introducing me to my first computer and then coaching me continuously and graciously for many years as to what computers are all about. Thank you, Ron, for devoting so much of your valuable, professional time in such an amiable and friendly way to my computer education.

Similar thanks to professional Multi-Media Producer, Tom Rincker, for his instant availability, in person or by telephone, and his recent weekly computer tutoring in exchange for Monday Night Football and a tray-dinner. Thank you, Tom, for your generosity of spirit and desire to make computers fun.

To Marjory Kron Lewi-Rucker, wife and helpmate. I am indebted to you, Marge for your continual listening and conversation about my writing activities, giving me new thoughts, and being the extraordinary life-friend you are. Thank you Marge.

OTHER BOOKS BY DOUG RUCKER

PERSONAL JOURNEY
How poetry forecast divorce

EARLY STORIES
Autobiography –1927 - 1950

GROUNDWORK
Autobiography – 1950 – 1064

GROWING EDGE
Autobiography – 1964 – 1970

BOOK OF WORDS
Sixty-seven homey essays

WHERE'S THE COOKIES AT?
Seventy-seven nonsensical essays and art

HAROLD AND THE ACID SEA OF REALITY
Sixty-eight essays on life

OFF THE WALL
24 artworks derived from graffiti

TRIAL BY FIRE
Autobiography - A tale of two houses

A BOOK ABOUT EVERYDAY STUFF
Poetic adventures with two dogs, Jorgie and Merle